THE COVENANT

Feb 1991
148 BE
To Mark
my true brother
love!
Weslie

The Covenant

Daily Readings from the Bahá'í Teachings

compiled by

ENOCH N. TANYI

GEORGE RONALD

OXFORD

GEORGE RONALD, Publisher
46 High Street, Kidlington, Oxford OX5 2DN

British Library Cataloguing in Publication Data

The Covenant : daily readings from the Baha'i teachings.
1. Bahaism.   Devotional works.
I. Tanyi, Enoch N.
297′8943

ISBN 0–85398–291–0
ISBN 0–85398–296–1 (Pbk)

Printed in Great Britain by
Billing & Sons Ltd, Worcester

Acknowledgements

Special thanks go to the Spiritual Assembly of the Bahá'ís of Yaoundé, Cameroon for generously providing the paper and offering their office facilities for the typing of the manuscript; to Alexander Agbor, Secretary of the National Spiritual Assembly of the Bahá'ís of Cameroon, for kindly allowing the National Assembly typist, Pauline Bessem, to do the typing; to Mr Prince Ayuk Kima, who made it possible to send the bulky manuscript to England at a time of economic crisis; to George Ronald, Publisher, and particularly to Wendi Momen, whose steady flow of letters and encouragement helped to keep my interest in this venture alive; and to my wife Mary, whose criticism about the slow pace with which I began this work spurred me on.

Introduction

In its letter of 2nd January 1986 to the Bahá'ís of the world, the Universal House of Justice declared the year 1992 a 'Holy Year'. During this year the Centenary of the Ascension of Bahá'u'lláh will be observed around the world by special commemorations and the inauguration of His Covenant will be celebrated in the City of the Covenant with the holding of the second Bahá'í World Congress.

The celebration of the inauguration of the Covenant of Bahá'u'lláh calls for a deep understanding of that Covenant. We need to focus our minds and hearts on its nature, its meaning and its unique features and to strengthen our dedication to it. We need to deepen our knowledge of both the Greater and the Lesser Covenants.

I have found that the best way to deepen on any subject is to read the Writings about that subject frequently and to meditate on them. It was to this end that I compiled *The Covenant: Daily Readings from the Bahá'í Teachings*.

Enoch Nyenti Tanyi
Limbé, Cameroon
Jamal 146
April 1989

This book is dedicated to the pioneers to and from Africa

The Covenant

A COVENANT in the religious sense is a binding agreement between God and man, whereby God requires of man certain behaviour in return for which He guarantees certain blessings, or whereby He gives man certain bounties in return for which He takes from those who accept them an undertaking to behave in a certain way. There is, for example, the Greater Covenant which every Manifestation of God makes with His followers, promising that in the fullness of time a new Manifestation will be sent, and taking from them the undertaking to accept Him when this occurs. There is also the Lesser Covenant that a Manifestation of God makes with His followers that they will accept His appointed successor after Him. If they do so, the Faith can remain united and pure, if not, the Faith becomes divided and its force spent. It is a Covenant of this kind that Bahá'u'lláh made with His followers regarding 'Abdu'l-Bahá and that 'Abdu'l-Bahá perpetuated through the Administrative Order.

Universal House of Justice
Letter to an individual believer, 23 March 1975

1

Bahá
(Splendour)

The Purpose of Religion

Naw-Rúz
Feast of Bahá

1 Bahá   *21 March*

RELIGION is verily the chief instrument for the establishment
of order in the world and of tranquillity amongst its peoples.

Bahá'u'lláh

2 Bahá   *22 March*

THE purpose of religion as revealed from the heaven of
God's holy Will is to establish unity and concord amongst
the peoples of the world; make it not the cause of dissension
and strife. The religion of God and His divine law are the
most potent instruments and the surest of all means for the
dawning of the light of unity amongst men. The progress of
the world, the development of nations, the tranquillity of
peoples, and the peace of all who dwell on earth are among
the principles and ordinances of God. Religion bestoweth
upon man the most precious of all gifts, offereth the cup of
prosperity, imparteth eternal life, and showereth imperishable benefits upon mankind.

Bahá'u'lláh

3 Bahá   23 March

THE purpose underlying the revelation of every heavenly Book, nay, of every divinely-revealed verse, is to endue all men with righteousness and understanding, so that peace and tranquillity may be firmly established amongst them. Whatsoever instilleth assurance into the hearts of men, whatsoever exalteth their station or promoteth their contentment, is acceptable in the sight of God. How lofty is the station which man, if he but choose to fulfil his high destiny, can attain!

Bahá'u'lláh

4 Bahá   24 March

THE Purpose of the one true God, exalted be His glory, in revealing Himself unto men is to lay bare those gems that lie hidden within the mine of their true and inmost selves.

Bahá'u'lláh

5 Bahá   25 March

AND now concerning thy question regarding the nature of religion. Know thou that they who are truly wise have likened the world unto the human temple. As the body of man needeth a garment to clothe it, so the body of mankind must needs be adorned with the mantle of justice and wisdom. Its robe is the Revelation vouchsafed unto it by God. Whenever this robe hath fulfilled its purpose, the Almighty will assuredly renew it. For every age requireth a fresh measure of the light of God. Every Divine Revelation hath been sent down in a manner that befitted the circumstances of the age in which it hath appeared.

Bahá'u'lláh

6 Bahá   26 March

IN truth, religion is a radiant light and an impregnable stronghold for the protection and welfare of the peoples of the world, for the fear of God impelleth man to hold fast to that which is good, and shun all evil. Should the lamp of religion be obscured, chaos and confusion will ensue, and the lights of fairness and justice, of tranquillity and peace cease to shine. Unto this will bear witness every man of true understanding.

Bahá'u'lláh

7 Bahá   27 March

THE purpose of all the divine religions is the establishment of the bonds of love and fellowship among men, and the heavenly phenomena of the revealed Word of God are intended to be a source of knowledge and illumination to humanity.

'Abdu'l-Bahá

8 Bahá   28 March

WHAT, then, is the mission of the divine Prophets? Their mission is the education and advancement of the world of humanity. They are the real Teachers and Educators, the universal Instructors of mankind.

'Abdu'l-Bahá

9 Bahá   29 March

IN further consideration of this subject, I wish you to be fair and reasonable in your judgement, setting aside all religious prejudices. We should earnestly seek and thoroughly investigate realities, recognizing that the purpose of the religion of God is the education of humanity and the unity and fellowship of mankind. Furthermore, we will establish the point that the foundations of the religions of God are one foundation. This foundation is not multiple, for it is reality itself. Reality does not admit of multiplicity, although each of the divine religions is separable into two divisions. One concerns the world of morality and the ethical training of human nature. It is directed to the advancement of the world of humanity in general; it reveals and inculcates the knowledge of God and makes possible the discovery of the verities of life. This is ideal and spiritual teaching, the essential quality of divine religion, and not subject to change or transformation. It is the one foundation of all the religions of God. Therefore, the religions are essentially one and the same.

'Abdu'l-Bahá

10 Bahá   30 March

. . . in the kingdoms of earth and heaven there must needs be manifested a Being, an Essence Who shall act as a

Manifestation and Vehicle for the transmission of the grace of the Divinity Itself, the Sovereign Lord of all. Through the Teachings of this Day Star of Truth every man will advance and develop until he attaineth the station at which he can manifest all the potential forces with which his inmost true self hath been endowed. It is for this very purpose that in every age and dispensation the Prophets of God and His chosen Ones have appeared amongst men, and have evinced such power as is born of God and such might as only the Eternal can reveal.

Bahá'u'lláh

11 Bahá   31 March

MEN at all times and under all conditions stand in need of one to exhort them, guide them and to instruct and teach them. Therefore He hath sent forth His Messengers, His Prophets and chosen ones that they might acquaint the people with the divine purpose underlying the revelation of Books and the raising up of Messengers, and that everyone may become aware of the trust of God which is latent in the reality of every soul.

Bahá'u'lláh

12 Bahá   1 April

THE Divine Messengers have been sent down, and their Books were revealed, for the purpose of promoting the knowledge of God, and of furthering unity and fellowship amongst men.

Bahá'u'lláh

13 Bahá   2 April

THE purpose of the one true God in manifesting Himself is to summon all mankind to truthfulness and sincerity, to piety and trustworthiness, to resignation and submissiveness to the Will of God, to forbearance and kindliness, to uprightness and wisdom. His object is to array every man with the mantle of a saintly character, and to adorn him with the ornament of holy and goodly deeds.

Bahá'u'lláh

14 Bahá   3 April

THEREFORE, it is evident that God has destined and intended religion to be the cause and means of cooperative effort and accomplishment among mankind. To this end He has sent the Prophets of God, the holy Manifestations of the Word, in order that the fundamental reality and religion of God may prove to be the bond of human unity, for the divine religions revealed by these holy Messengers have one and the same foundation. All will admit, therefore, that the divine religions are intended to be the means of true human cooperation, that they are united in the purpose of making humanity one family, for they rest upon the universal foundation of love, and love is the first effulgence of Divinity.

'Abdu'l-Bahá

15 Bahá   4 April

THE divine Manifestations since the day of Adam have striven to unite humanity so that all may be accounted as one soul. The function and purpose of a shepherd is to gather and not disperse his flock. The Prophets of God have been divine Shepherds of humanity. They have established a bond of love and unity among mankind, made scattered peoples one nation and wandering tribes a mighty kingdom. They have laid the foundation of the oneness of God and summoned all to universal peace. All these holy, divine Manifestations are one. They have served one God, promulgated the same truth, founded the same institutions and reflected the same light. Their appearances have been successive and correlated; each One has announced and extolled the One Who was to follow, and all laid the foundation of reality. They summoned and invited the people to love and made the human world a mirror of the Word of God. Therefore, the divine religions They established have one foundation; Their teachings, proofs and evidences are one; in name and form They differ, but in reality They agree and are the same.

'Abdu'l-Bahá

16 Bahá   5 April

EVERY Prophet Whom the Almighty and Peerless Creator hath purposed to send to the peoples of the earth hath been entrusted with a Message, and charged to act in a manner that would best meet the requirements of the age in which He appeared. God's purpose in sending His Prophets unto men is twofold. The first is to liberate the children of men from the darkness of ignorance, and guide them to the light of true understanding. The second is to ensure the peace and tranquillity of mankind, and to provide all the means by which they can be established.

Bahá'u'lláh

17 Bahá   6 April

THE Lord of mankind has caused His holy, divine Manifestations to come into the world. He has revealed His heavenly Books in order to establish spiritual brotherhood and through the power of the Holy Spirit has made it practicable for perfect fraternity to be realized among mankind. And when through the breaths of the Holy Spirit this perfect fraternity and agreement are established amongst men – this brotherhood and love being spiritual in character, this loving kindness being heavenly, these constraining bonds being divine – a unity appears which is indissoluble, unchanging and never subject to transformation. It is ever the same and will forever remain the same.

'Abdu'l-Bahá

18 Bahá   7 April

ALL the Divine Manifestations sent by God into the world would have gone through their terrible hardships and sufferings for the single hope of spreading Truth, unity and concord among men.

'Abdu'l-Bahá

19 Bahá   8 April

KNOW thou assuredly that the essence of all the Prophets of God is one and the same. Their unity is absolute. God, the Creator, saith: There is no distinction whatsoever among the Bearers of My Message. They all have but one purpose; their secret is the same secret. To prefer one in honour to another, to exalt certain ones above the rest, is in no wise to be permitted. Every true Prophet hath regarded His Message as fundamentally the same as the Revelation of every other Prophet gone before Him.

Bahá'u'lláh

The month of Jalál begins at sunset.

2

Jalál
(Glory)

The Greater Covenant

Feast of Jalál

1 Jalál   *9 April*

THE Lord of the universe hath never raised up a prophet nor
hath He sent down a Book unless He hath established His
covenant with all men, calling for their acceptance of the
next Revelation and of the next Book; inasmuch as the
outpourings of His bounty are ceaseless and without limit.

The Báb

2 Jalál   *10 April*

THY Lord hath never raised up a prophet in the past who
failed to summon the people to His Lord, and today is truly
similar to the times of old, were ye to ponder over the verses
revealed by God.

The Báb

3 Jalál   *11 April*

WHY is it that the advent of every true Manifestation of God hath been accompanied by such strife and tumult, by such tyranny and upheaval? This notwithstanding the fact that all the Prophets of God, whenever made manifest unto the peoples of the world, have invariably foretold the coming of yet another Prophet after them, and have established such signs as would herald the advent of the future Dispensation. To this the records of all sacred books bear witness. Why then is it that despite the expectation of men in their quest of the Manifestations of Holiness, and in spite of the signs recorded in the sacred books, should such acts of violence, of oppression and cruelty, have been perpetrated in every age and cycle against all the Prophets and chosen Ones of God?

Bahá'u'lláh

4 Jalál   12 April

. . . know thou that the First Remembrance, which is the Primal Will of God, may be likened unto the sun. God hath created Him through the potency of His might, and He hath, from the beginning that hath no beginning, caused Him to be manifested in every Dispensation through the compelling power of His behest, and God will, to the end that knoweth no end, continue to manifest Him according to the good-pleasure of His invincible Purpose.

And know thou that He indeed resembleth the sun. Were the risings of the sun to continue till the end that hath no end, yet there hath not been nor ever will be more than one sun; and were its settings to endure for evermore, still there hath not been nor ever will be more than one sun. It is this Primal Will which appeareth resplendent in every Prophet and speaketh forth in every revealed Book. It knoweth no beginning, inasmuch as the First deriveth its firstness from

18

It; and knoweth no end, for the Last oweth its lastness unto
It.

The Báb

5 *Jalál* ✗ *13 April*

IN the time of the First Manifestation the Primal Will
appeared in Adam; in the day of Noah It became known in
Noah; in the day of Abraham in Him; and so in the day of
Moses; the day of Jesus; the day of Muḥammad, the Apostle
of God; the day of the 'Point of the Bayán'; the day of Him
Whom God shall make manifest; and the day of the One
Who will appear after Him Whom God shall make manifest.
Hence the inner meaning of the words uttered by the
Apostle of God, 'I am all the Prophets', inasmuch as what
shineth resplendent in each one of Them hath been and will
ever remain the one and the same sun.

The Báb

6 *Jalál* *14 April*

THE revelation of the Divine Reality hath everlastingly been
identical with its concealment and its concealment identical
with its revelation. That which is intended by 'Revelation of
God' is the Tree of divine Truth that betokeneth none but
Him, and it is this divine Tree that hath raised and will raise
up Messengers, and hath revealed and will ever reveal
Scriptures. From eternity unto eternity this Tree of divine
Truth hath served and will ever serve as the throne of the
revelation and concealment of God among His creatures,
and in every age is made manifest through whomsoever He
pleaseth. At the time of the revelation of the Qur'án He

asserted His transcendent power through the advent of Muḥammad, and on the occasion of the revelation of the Bayán He demonstrated His sovereign might through the appearance of the Point of the Bayán, and when Him Whom God shall make manifest will shine forth, it will be through Him that He will vindicate the truth of His Faith, as He pleaseth, with whatsoever He pleaseth and for whatsoever He pleaseth. He is with all things, yet nothing is with Him. He is not within a thing nor above it nor beside it. Any reference to His being established upon the throne implieth that the Exponent of His Revelation is established upon the seat of transcendent authority . . .

The Báb

7 *Jalál*   15 *April*

CONTEMPLATE with thine inward eye the chain of successive Revelations that hath linked the Manifestation of Adam with that of the Báb. I testify before God that each one of these Manifestations hath been sent down through the operation of the Divine Will and Purpose, that each hath been the bearer of a specific Message, that each hath been entrusted with a divinely-revealed Book and been commissioned to unravel the mysteries of a mighty Tablet. The measure of the Revelation with which every one of them hath been identified had been definitely fore-ordained. This, verily, is a token of Our favour unto them, if ye be of those that comprehend this truth.

Bahá'u'lláh

8 *Jalál*   16 *April*

HIS Holiness Abraham, on Him be peace, made a covenant

concerning His Holiness Moses and gave the glad-tidings of His coming. His Holiness Moses made a covenant concerning the Promised One, i.e. His Holiness Christ, and announced the good news of His Manifestation to the world. His Holiness Christ made a covenant concerning the Paraclete and gave the tidings of His coming. His Holiness the Prophet Muḥammad made a covenant concerning His Holiness the Báb and the Báb was the One promised by Muḥammad, for Muḥammad gave the tidings of His coming. The Báb made a Covenant concerning the Blessed Beauty of Bahá'u'lláh and gave the glad-tidings of His coming for the Blessed Beauty was the One promised by His Holiness the Báb. Bahá'u'lláh made a covenant concerning a promised One who will become manifest after one thousand or thousands of years.

'Abdu'l-Bahá

9 Jalál   17 April

... the Revelation of God may be likened to the sun. No matter how innumerable its risings, there is but one sun, and upon it depends the life of all things. It is clear and evident that the object of all preceding Dispensations hath been to pave the way for the advent of Muḥammad, the Apostle of God. These, including the Muḥammadan Dispensation, have had, in their turn, as their objective the Revelation proclaimed by the Qá'im. The purpose underlying this Revelation, as well as those that preceded it, has, in like manner, been to announce the advent of the Faith of Him Whom God will make manifest. And this Faith – the Faith of Him Whom God will make manifest – in its turn, together with all the Revelations gone before it, have as their object the Manifestation destined to succeed it. And the latter, no

21

less than all the Revelations preceding it, prepare the way for the Revelation which is yet to follow. The process of the rise and setting of the Sun of Truth will thus indefinitely continue – a process that hath had no beginning and will have no end.

Well is it with him who in every Dispensation recognizeth the Purpose of God for that Dispensation, and is not deprived therefrom by turning his gaze towards the things of the past.

The Báb

10 Jalál   18 April

THE divine religions are like the progression of the seasons of the year. When the earth becomes dead and desolate and because of frost and cold no trace of vanished spring remains, the springtime dawns again and clothes everything with a new garment of life. The meadows become fresh and green, the trees are adorned with verdure and fruits appear upon them. Then the winter comes again, and all the traces of spring disappear. This is the continuous cycle of the seasons – spring, winter, then the return of spring. But though the calendar changes and the years move forward, each springtime that comes is the return of the springtime that has gone; this spring is the renewal of the former spring. Springtime is springtime, no matter when or how often it comes. The divine Prophets are as the coming of spring, each renewing and quickening the teachings of the Prophet Who came before Him. Just as all seasons of spring are essentially one as to newness of life, vernal showers and beauty, so the essence of the mission and accomplishment of all the Prophets is one and the same.

'Abdu'l-Bahá

22

11 Jalál   19 April

. . . it is a basic principle of the Law of God that in every Prophetic Mission, He entereth into a Covenant with all believers – a Covenant that endureth until the end of that Mission, until the promised day when the Personage stipulated at the outset of the Mission is made manifest. Consider Moses, He Who conversed with God. Verily, upon Mount Sinai, Moses entered into a Covenant regarding the Messiah, with all those souls who would live in the day of the Messiah. And those souls, although they appeared many centuries after Moses, were nevertheless – so far as the Covenant, which is outside time, was concerned – present there with Moses.

'Abdu'l-Bahá

12 Jalál   20 April

. . . the Prophets of old, each and every one, whenever announcing to the people of their day the advent of the coming Revelation, have invariably and specifically referred to that sovereignty with which the promised Manifestation must needs be invested. This is attested by the records of the scriptures of the past. This sovereignty hath not been solely and exclusively attributed to the Qá'im. Nay rather, the attribute of sovereignty and all other names and attributes of God have been and will ever be vouchsafed unto all the Manifestations of God, before and after Him, inasmuch as these Manifestations, as it hath already been explained, are the Embodiments of the attributes of God, the Invisible, and the Revealers of the divine mysteries.

Bahá'u'lláh

The Feast of Riḍván begins at sunset.

23

First Day of Riḍván

A PRAISE which is exalted above every mention or description beseemeth the Adored One, the Possessor of all things visible and invisible, Who hath enabled the Primal Point to reveal countless Books and Epistles and Who, through the potency of His sublime Word, hath called into being the entire creation, whether of the former or more recent generations. Moreover He hath in every age and cycle, in conformity with His transcendent wisdom, sent forth a divine Messenger to revive the dispirited and despondent souls with the living waters of His utterance, One Who is indeed the Expounder, the true Interpreter, inasmuch as man is unable to comprehend that which hath streamed forth from the Pen of Glory and is recorded in His heavenly Books. Men at all times and under all conditions stand in need of one to exhort them, guide them and to instruct and teach them.

Bahá'u'lláh

24

14 Jalál   22 April

ALL the Prophets are the Temples of the Cause of God, Who have appeared clothed in divers attire. If thou wilt observe with discriminating eyes, thou wilt behold Them all abiding in the same tabernacle, soaring in the same heaven, seated upon the same throne, uttering the same speech, and proclaiming the same Faith. Such is the unity of those Essences of Being, those Luminaries of infinite and im-measurable splendour! Wherefore, should one of these Manifestations of Holiness proclaim saying: 'I am the return of all the Prophets', He, verily, speaketh the truth. In like manner, in every subsequent Revelation, the return of the former Revelation is a fact, the truth of which is firmly established.

Bahá'u'lláh

15 Jalál   23 April

FROM time immemorial the divine teachings have been successively revealed, and the bounties of the Holy Spirit have ever been emanating. All the teachings are one reality, for reality is single and does not admit multiplicity. There-fore, the divine Prophets are one, inasmuch as They reveal the one reality, the Word of God. Abraham announced teachings founded upon reality, Moses proclaimed reality, Christ established reality and Bahá'u'lláh was the Messenger and Herald of reality.

'Abdu'l-Bahá

16 Jalál   24 April

THE holy Manifestations Who have been the Sources or

Founders of the various religious systems were united and agreed in purpose and teaching. Abraham, Moses, Zoroaster, Buddha, Jesus, Muḥammad, the Báb and Bahá'u'lláh are one in spirit and reality. Moreover, each Prophet fulfilled the promise of the One Who came before Him and, likewise, each announced the One Who would follow. Consider how Abraham foretold the coming of Moses, and Moses embodied the Abrahamic statement. Moses prophesied the Messianic cycle, and Christ fulfilled the law of Moses. It is evident, therefore, that the Holy Manifestations Who founded the religious systems are united and agreed; there is no differentiation possible in Their mission and teachings; all are reflectors of reality, and all are promulgators of the religion of God. The divine religion is reality, and reality is not multiple; it is one.

'Abdu'l-Bahá

17 Jalál   25 April

THE Sun of Divinity and of Reality has revealed itself in various mirrors. Though these mirrors are many, yet the Sun is one. The bestowals of God are one; the reality of the divine religion is one. Consider how one and the same light has reflected itself in the different mirrors or manifestations of it. There are certain souls who are lovers of the Sun; they perceive the effulgence of the Sun from every mirror. They are not fettered or attached to the mirrors; they are attached to the Sun itself and adore it, no matter from what point it may shine. But those who adore the mirror and are attached to it become deprived of witnessing the light of the Sun when it shines forth from another mirror.

'Abdu'l-Bahá

18 Jalál   26 April

THE divine Manifestations have been iconoclastic in Their teachings, uprooting error, destroying false religious beliefs and summoning mankind anew to the fundamental oneness of God. All of Them have, likewise, proclaimed the oneness of the world of humanity. The essential teaching of Moses was the law of Sinai, the Ten Commandments. Christ renewed and again revealed the commands of the one God and precepts of human action. In Muḥammad, although the circle was wider, the intention of His teaching was likewise to uplift and unify humanity in the knowledge of the one God. In the Báb the circle was again very much enlarged, but the essential teaching was the same. The Books of Bahá'u'lláh number more than one hundred. Each one is an evident proof sufficient for mankind; each one from foundation to apex proclaims the essential unity of God and humanity, the love of God, the abolition of war and the divine standard of peace. Each one also inculcates divine morality, the manifestation of lordly graces – in every word a book of meanings. For the Word of God is collective wisdom, absolute knowledge and eternal truth.

'Abdu'l-Bahá

19 Jalál   27 April

FOR instance, if all those who were expecting the fulfilment of the promise of Jesus had been assured of the manifestation of Muḥammad, the Apostle of God, not one would have turned aside from the sayings of Jesus. So likewise in the Revelation of the Point of the Bayán, if all should be assured that this is that same Promised Mihdí [One Who is guided] whom the Apostle of God foretold, not one of the believers in the Qur'án would turn aside from the sayings of the Apostle of God. So likewise in the Revelation of Him Whom God shall make manifest, behold the same thing; for should all be assured that He is that same 'He Whom God shall make manifest' whom the Point of the Bayán hath foretold, not one would turn aside.

The Báb

The month of Jamál begins at sunset.

3

Jamál
(Beauty)

The Covenant of the Báb

Feast of Jamál

1 Jamál   *28 April*

WITH each and every Prophet Whom We have sent down in the past, We have established a separate Covenant concerning the Remembrance of God and His Day. Manifest, in the realm of glory and through the power of truth, are the Remembrance of God and His Day before the eyes of the angels that circle His mercy-seat.

The Báb

The commemoration of the Ninth Day of Riḍván begins at sunset.

Ninth Day of Riḍván

2 Jamál   *29 April*

GLORIFIED art Thou, O My God! Bear Thou witness that, through this Book, I have covenanted with all created things concerning the Mission of Him Whom Thou shalt make manifest, ere the covenant concerning Mine own Mission had been established.

The Báb

3 Jamál   30 April

IF ye seek God, it behooveth you to seek Him Whom God shall make manifest, and if ye cherish the desire to dwell in the Ark of Names, ye will be distinguished as the guides·to Him Whom God shall make manifest, did ye but believe in Him. Verily then make your hearts the day-springs of His exalted Names as recorded in the Book, and ye shall, even as mirrors placed before the sun, be able to receive enlightenment.

The Báb

4 Jamál   1 May

RECOGNIZE Him by His verses. The greater your neglect in seeking to know Him, the more grievously will ye be veiled in fire.

The Báb

The commemoration of the Twelfth Day of Riḍván begins at sunset.

Twelfth Day of Riḍván

5 Jamál   2 May

WELL is it with him who fixeth his gaze upon the Order of Bahá'u'lláh and rendereth thanks unto His Lord! For He will assuredly be made manifest. God hath indeed irrevocably ordained it in the Bayán.

The Báb

6 Jamál   3 May

I, VERILY, am a believer in Him, and in His Faith, and in His Book, and in His Testimonies, and in His Ways, and in all that proceedeth from Him concerning them. I glory in My kinship with Him, and pride Myself on My belief in Him.

The Báb

7 Jamál   4 May

THE glory of Him Whom God shall make manifest is immeasurably above every other glory, and His majesty is far above every other majesty. His beauty excelleth every other embodiment of beauty, and His grandeur immensely exceedeth every other manifestation of grandeur. Every light paleth before the radiance of His light, and every other exponent of mercy falleth short before the tokens of His mercy. Every other perfection is as naught in face of His consummate perfection, and every other display of might is as nothing before His absolute might. His names are superior to all other names. His good-pleasure taketh precedence over any other expression of good-pleasure. His pre-eminent exaltation is far above the reach of every other symbol of exaltation. The splendour of His appearance far surpasseth that of any other appearance. His divine concealment is far more profound than any other concealment. His loftiness is immeasurably above every other loftiness. His gracious favour is unequalled by any other evidence of favour. His power transcendeth every power. His sovereignty is invincible in the face of every other sovereignty. His celestial dominion is exalted far above every other dominion. His knowledge pervadeth all created things, and His consummate power extendeth over all beings.

The Báb

8 Jamál   5 May

THE Bayán deriveth all its glory from 'Him Whom God shall make manifest'.

The Báb

9 Jamál   6 May

BETTER is it for a person to write down but one of His verses than to transcribe the whole of the Bayán and all the books which have been written in the Dispensation of the Bayán. For everything shall be set aside except His Writings, which will endure until the following Revelation. And should anyone inscribe with true faith but one letter of that Revelation, his recompense would be greater than for inscribing all the heavenly Writings of the past and all that has been written during previous Dispensations. Likewise continue thou to ascend through one Revelation after another, knowing that thy progress in the Knowledge of God shall never come to an end, even as it can have no beginning.

The Báb

10 Jamál   7 May

BETTER is it for thee to recite but one of the verses of Him Whom God shall make manifest than to set down the whole of the Bayán, for on that Day that one verse can save thee, whereas the entire Bayán cannot save thee.

The Báb

11 Jamál   8 May

I SWEAR by the most holy Essence of God – exalted and

glorified be He – that in the Day of the appearance of Him Whom God shall make manifest a thousand perusals of the Bayán cannot equal the perusal of a single verse to be revealed by Him Whom God shall make manifest.

The Báb

12 Jamál   9 May

AND know thou of a certainty that every letter revealed in the Bayán is solely intended to evoke submission unto Him Whom God shall make manifest, for it is He Who hath revealed the Bayán prior to His Own manifestation.

The Báb

13 Jamál   10 May

SUFFER not yourselves to be shut out as by a veil from God after He hath revealed Himself. For all that hath been exalted in the Bayán is but as a ring upon My hand, and I Myself am, verily, but a ring upon the hand of Him Whom God shall make manifest – glorified be His mention! He turneth it as He pleaseth, for whatsoever He pleaseth, and through whatsoever He pleaseth. He verily is the Help in Peril, the Most High.

The Báb

14 Jamál   11 May

AT the time of the appearance of Him Whom God shall make manifest, wert thou to perform thy deeds for the sake of the Point of the Bayán, they would be regarded as performed for one other than God, inasmuch as on that Day the Point of the Bayán is none other than Him Whom God shall make manifest . . .

The Báb

15 Jamál   12 May

WE have planted the Garden of the Bayán in the name of Him Whom God will make manifest, and have granted you permission to live therein until the time of His manifestation; then from the moment the Cause of Him Whom God will make manifest is inaugurated, We forbid you all the things ye hold as your own, unless ye may, by the leave of your Lord, be able to regain possession thereof.

The Báb

16 Jamál   13 May

IT behooveth you to await the Day of the appearance of Him Whom God shall manifest. Indeed My aim in planting the Tree of the Bayán hath been none other than to enable you to recognize Me. In truth I Myself am the first to bow down before God and to believe in Him. Therefore let not your recognition become fruitless, inasmuch as the Bayán, notwithstanding the sublimity of its station, beareth fealty to Him Whom God shall make manifest, and it is He Who beseemeth most to be acclaimed as the Seat of divine Reality, though indeed He is I and I am He. However, when the Tree of the Bayán attaineth its highest development, We shall bend it low as a token of adoration towards its Lord Who will appear in the person of Him Whom God shall make manifest. Perchance ye may be privileged to glorify God as it befitteth His august Self.

The Báb

17 Jamál   14 May

THE light of the people of the world is their knowledge and utterance; while the splendours shed from the glorious acts of Him Whom God shall make manifest are His Words, through whose potency He rolleth up the whole world of existence, sets it under His Own authority by relating it unto Himself, then as the Mouthpiece of God, the Source of His divine light – exalted and glorified be He – proclaimeth: 'Verily, verily, I am God, no God is there but Me; in truth all others except Me are My creatures. Say, O My creatures! Me alone, therefore, should ye fear'.

The Báb

18 Jamál   15 May

WHEN the Day-Star of Bahá will shine resplendent above the horizon of eternity it is incumbent upon you to present yourselves before His Throne. Beware lest ye be seated in His presence or ask questions without His leave. Fear ye God, O concourse of the Mirrors.

Beg ye of Him the wondrous tokens of His favour that He may graciously reveal for you whatever He willeth and desireth, inasmuch as on that Day all the revelations of divine bounty shall circle around the Seat of His glory and emanate from His presence, could ye but understand it.

The Báb

19 Jamál   16 May

O SERVANTS of God! Be ye patient, for, God grant, He Who is the sovereign Truth will suddenly appear amongst you, invested with the power of the mighty Word, and ye shall then be confounded by the Truth itself, and ye shall have no power to ward it off; and verily I am a witness over all mankind.

The Báb

The month of 'Aẓamat begins at sunset.

4

'Aẓamat
(Grandeur)

Bahá'u'lláh: The Promise Fulfilled

Feast of 'Aẓamat

1 'Aẓamat   *17 May*

GLORIFIED art Thou, O Lord my God! Look Thou upon this wronged one, who hath been sorely afflicted by the oppressors among Thy creatures and the infidels among Thine enemies, though he himself hath refused to breathe a single breath but by Thy leave and at Thy bidding. I lay asleep on my couch, O my God, when lo, the gentle winds of Thy grace and Thy loving-kindness passed over me, and wakened me through the power of Thy sovereignty and Thy gifts, and bade me arise before Thy servants, and speak forth Thy praise, and glorify Thy word. Thereupon most of Thy people reviled me. I swear by Thy glory, O my God! I never thought that they would show forth such deeds, aware as I am that Thou hast Thyself announced this Revelation unto them in the Scrolls of Thy commandment and the Tablets of Thy decree, and hast covenanted with them concerning this youth in every word sent down by Thee unto Thy creatures and Thy people.

Bahá'u'lláh

41

2 'Aẓamat   18 May

O MY friend! The undying Fire which the Lord of the
Kingdom hath kindled in the midst of the holy Tree is
burning fiercely in the midmost heart of the world. The
conflagration it will provoke will envelop the whole earth.
Its blazing flames will illuminate its peoples and kindreds.
All the signs have been revealed; every prophetic allusion
hath been manifested. Whatever hath been enshrined in all
the Scriptures of the past hath been made evident. To doubt
or hesitate is no more possible . . . Time is pressing. The
Divine Charger is impatient, and can tarry no longer.

Bahá'u'lláh

3 'Aẓamat   19 May

THE Revelation which, from time immemorial, hath been
acclaimed as the Purpose and Promise of all the Prophets of
God, and the most cherished Desire of His Messengers, hath
now, by virtue of the pervasive Will of the Almighty and at
His irresistible bidding, been revealed unto men. The advent
of such a Revelation hath been heralded in all the sacred
Scriptures.

Bahá'u'lláh

4 'Aẓamat   20 May

IN this most mighty Revelation all the Dispensations of the
past have attained their highest, their final consummation.

Bahá'u'lláh

5 'Aẓamat 21 May

AND when Thou didst purpose to make Thyself known unto
men, Thou didst successively reveal the Manifestations of
Thy Cause, and ordained each to be a sign of Thy
Revelation among Thy people, and the Day-Spring of Thine
invisible Self amidst Thy creatures, until the time when, as
decreed by Thee, all Thy previous Revelations culminated in
Him Whom Thou hast appointed as the Lord of all who are
in the heaven of revelation and the kingdom of creation,
Him Whom Thou hast established as the Sovereign Lord of
all who are in the heavens and all who are on the earth. He it
was Whom Thou hast determined to be the Herald of Thy
Most Great Revelation and the Announcer of Thy Most
Ancient Splendour. In this Thou hadst no other purpose
except to try them who have manifested Thy most excellent
titles unto all who are in heaven and on earth. He it was
Whom Thou hast commanded to establish His covenant with
all created things.

Bahá'u'lláh

6 'Aẓamat 22 May

FEAR ye God and breathe not a word concerning His Most
Great Remembrance other than what hath been ordained by
God, inasmuch as We have established a separate covenant
regarding Him with every Prophet and His followers.
Indeed, We have not sent any Messenger without this
binding covenant and We do not, of a truth, pass judgement
upon anything except after the covenant of Him Who is the
Supreme Gate hath been established. Ere long the veil shall
be lifted from your eyes at the appointed time. Ye shall then

43

behold the sublime Remembrance of God, unclouded and vivid.

The Báb

The anniversary of the Declaration of the Báb is observed at two hours after sunset on this day.

Declaration of the Báb

7 'Aẓamat   23 May

THIS is the Day, O my Lord, which Thou didst announce unto all mankind as the Day whereon Thou wouldst reveal Thy Self, and shed Thy radiance, and shine brightly over all Thy creatures. Thou hast, moreover, entered into a covenant with them, in Thy Books, and Thy Scriptures, and Thy Scrolls, and Thy Tablets, concerning Him Who is the Day-Spring of Thy Revelation, and hast appointed the Bayán to be the Herald of this Most Great and all-glorious Manifestation, and this most resplendent and most sublime Appearance.

Bahá'u'lláh

8 'Aẓamat   24 May

I TESTIFY before God to the greatness, the inconceivable greatness of this Revelation. Again and again have We in most of Our Tablets borne witness to this truth, that mankind may be roused from its heedlessness. In this most mighty Revelation all the Dispensations of the past have attained their highest, their final consummation. That which

44

hath been made manifest in this pre-eminent, this most exalted Revelation, stands unparalleled in the annals of the past, nor will future ages witness its like. He it is Who in the Old Testament hath been named Jehovah, Who in the Gospel hath been designated as the Spirit of Truth, and in the Qur'án acclaimed as the Great Announcement. But for Him no Divine Messenger would have been invested with the robe of prophethood, nor would any of the sacred Scriptures have been revealed. To this bear witness all created things. The word which the one true God uttereth in this day, though that word be the most familiar and commonplace of terms, is invested with supreme, with unique distinction. The generality of mankind is still immature. Had it acquired sufficient capacity We would have bestowed upon it so great a measure of Our knowledge that all who dwell on earth and in heaven would have found themselves, by virtue of the grace streaming from Our Pen, completely independent of all knowledge save the knowledge of God, and would have been securely established upon the throne of abiding tranquillity.

Bahá'u'lláh

9 'Aẓamat   25 May

THE time fore-ordained unto the peoples and kindreds of the earth is now come. The promises of God, as recorded in the holy Scriptures, have all been fulfilled. Out of Zion hath gone forth the Law of God, and Jerusalem, and the hills and land thereof, are filled with the glory of His Revelation. Happy is the man that pondereth in his heart that which hath been revealed in the Books of God, the Help in Peril, the Self-Subsisting. Meditate upon this, O ye Beloved of God, and let your ears be attentive unto His Word, so that ye may, by His grace and mercy, drink your fill from the crystal waters of constancy, and become as steadfast and immovable as the mountain in His Cause.

Bahá'u'lláh

10 'Aẓamat   26 May

GOD testifieth that there is none other God but Him and that He Who hath appeared is the Hidden Mystery, the Treasured Symbol, the Most Great Book for all peoples, and the Heaven of bounty for the whole world. He is the Most Mighty Sign amongst men and the Dayspring of the most august attributes in the realm of creation. Through Him hath appeared that which had been hidden from time immemorial and been veiled from the eyes of men. He is the One Whose Manifestation was announced by the heavenly Scriptures, in former times and more recently. Whoso acknowledgeth belief in Him and in His signs and testimonies hath in truth acknowledged that which the Tongue of Grandeur uttered ere the creation of earth and heaven and the revelation of the Kingdom of Names. Through Him the ocean of knowledge hath surged amidst mankind and the river of divine wisdom hath gushed out at the behest of God, the Lord of Days.

Bahá'u'lláh

11 'Aẓamat   27 May

THE river Jordan is joined to the Most Great Ocean, and the Son, in the holy vale, crieth out: 'Here am I, here am I, O Lord, my God!', whilst Sinai circleth round the House, and the Burning Bush calleth aloud: 'He Who is the Desired One is come in His transcendent majesty.' Say, Lo! The Father is come, and that which ye were promised in the Kingdom is fulfilled! This is the Word which the Son concealed, when to those around Him He said: 'Ye cannot bear it now.' And when the appointed time was fulfilled and the Hour had struck, the Word shone forth above the horizon of the Will of God. Beware, O followers of the Son, that ye cast it not behind your backs. Take ye fast hold of it. Better is this for you than all that ye possess.

Bahá'u'lláh

12 'Aẓamat   28 May

GOD testifieth that there is none other God but Him and that He Who hath come from the heaven of divine revelation is the Hidden Secret, the Impenetrable Mystery, Whose advent hath been foretold in the Book of God and hath been heralded by His Prophets and Messengers. Through Him the mysteries have been unravelled, the veils rent asunder and the signs and evidences disclosed. Lo! He hath now been made manifest. He bringeth to light whatsoever He willeth, and treadeth upon the high places of the earth, invested with transcendent majesty and power.

Bahá'u'lláh

The commemoration of the Ascension of Bahá'u'lláh begins at sunset.

Ascension of Bahá'u'lláh

13 'Aẓamat   29 May

IN Thy holy Books, in Thy Scriptures and Thy Scrolls Thou

THE COVENANT

hast promised all the peoples of the world that Thou Thyself
shalt appear and shalt remove the veils of glory from Thy
face . . .

I bear witness that Thou hast in truth fulfilled Thy pledge
and hast made manifest the One Whose advent was foretold
by Thy Prophets, Thy chosen ones and by them that serve
Thee. He hath come from the heaven of glory and power,
bearing the banners of Thy signs and the standards of Thy
testimonies. Through the potency of Thine indomitable
power and strength, He stood up before the faces of all men
and summoned all mankind to the summit of transcendent
glory and unto the all-highest Horizon, in such wise that
neither the oppression of the ecclesiastics nor the onslaught
of the rulers was able to deter Him.

Bahá'u'lláh

*The anniversary of the Ascension of Bahá'u'lláh is observed at three
o'clock on the morning of this day.*

14 'Aẓamat   30 May

SAY, by the righteousness of God! The All-Merciful is come
invested with power and sovereignty. Through His potency
the foundations of religions have quaked and the Nightingale of Utterance hath warbled its melody upon the
highest branch of true understanding. Verily, He Who was
hidden in the knowledge of God and is mentioned in the
Holy Scriptures hath appeared.

Bahá'u'lláh

15 'Aẓamat   31 May

THE sole object of whatsoever My Previous Manifestation

48

and Harbinger of My beauty hath revealed hath been My
Revelation and the proclamation of My Cause. Never – and
to this He Who is the Sovereign Truth beareth Me witness –
would He have, but for Me, pronounced what He did
pronounce.

Bahá'u'lláh

16 'Aẓamat   1 June

THOU art He, O my Lord, Who hath, in every line of Thy
Book, entered into covenant with them for me, and made it
so sure that none of Thy creatures can any longer evade it.
Thou didst say – and Thy word is the truth: 'One single letter
from Him excelleth all that hath been sent down in the
Bayán.'

Bahá'u'lláh

17 'Aẓamat   2 June

WITH a detached heart, and a dilated breast, and an utterly
truthful tongue, recite thou these sublime words that have
been revealed by My Forerunner – the Primal Point. He
saith – glorified be His utterance – addressing his honour,
'Aẓím: 'This, verily, is the thing We promised thee, ere the
moment We answered thy call. Wait thou until nine will
have elapsed from the time of the Bayán. Then exclaim:
"Blessed, therefore, be God, the most excellent of Makers!"
Say: This, verily, is an Announcement which none except
God hath comprehended. Ye, however, will be unaware on
that day.' In the year nine this Most Great Revelation arose
and shone forth brightly above the horizon of the Will of
God. None can deny it save he who is heedless and

49

doubteth. We pray God to aid His servants to return unto Him, and beg forgiveness for the things they committed in this vain life. He, verily, is the Forgiving, the Pardoner, the All-Merciful.

Bahá'u'lláh

18 'Azamat   3 June

SAY: 'The light hath shone forth from the horizon of Revelation, and the whole earth hath been illumined at the coming of Him Who is the Lord of the Day of the Covenant!' The doubters have perished, whilst he that turned, guided by the light of assurance, unto the Dayspring of Certitude hath prospered.

Bahá'u'lláh

19 'Azamat   4 June

EVERY proof and prophecy, every manner of evidence, whether based on reason or on the text of the scriptures and traditions, are to be regarded as centred in the persons of Bahá'u'lláh and the Báb. In them is to be found their complete fulfilment.

'Abdu'l-Bahá

The month of Núr begins at sunset.

5

Núr
(Light)

The Greatness of this Day

Feast of Núr

1 Núr   5 June

ALL glory be to this Day, the Day in which the fragrances of
mercy have been wafted over all created things, a Day so
blest that past ages and centuries can never hope to rival it, a
Day in which the countenance of the Ancient of Days hath
turned towards His holy seat. Thereupon the voices of all
created things, and beyond them those of the Concourse on
High, were heard calling aloud: 'Haste thee, O Carmel, for
lo, the light of the countenance of God, the Ruler of the
Kingdom of Names and Fashioner of the heavens, hath been
lifted upon thee.'

Bahá'u'lláh

2 Núr   6 June

TAKE heed lest anything deter thee from extolling the
greatness of this Day – the Day whereon the Finger of
majesty and power hath opened the seal of the Wine of
Reunion, and called all who are in the heavens and all who
are on the earth. Preferrest thou to tarry when the breeze

announcing the Day of God hath already breathed over thee, or art thou of them that are shut out as by a veil from Him?

Bahá'u'lláh

3 Núr   7 June

SHOULD the greatness of this Day be revealed in its fullness, every man would forsake a myriad lives in his longing to partake, though it be for one moment, of its great glory – how much more this world and its corruptible treasures!

Bahá'u'lláh

4 Núr   8 June

THIS is the Day in which He Who held converse with God hath attained the light of the Ancient of Days, and quaffed the pure waters of reunion from this Cup that hath caused the seas to swell. Say: By the one true God! Sinai is circling round the Day Spring of Revelation, while from the heights of the Kingdom the Voice of the Spirit of God is heard proclaiming: 'Bestir yourselves, ye proud ones of the earth, and hasten ye unto Him.' Carmel hath, in this Day, hastened in longing adoration to attain His court, whilst from the heart of Zion there cometh the cry: 'The promise is fulfilled. That which had been announced in the holy Writ of God, the most Exalted, the Almighty, the Best-Beloved, is made manifest.'

Bahá'u'lláh

5 Núr   9 June

SAY: O men! This is a matchless Day. Matchless must,

likewise, be the tongue that celebrateth the praise of the Desire of all nations, and matchless the deed that aspireth to be acceptable in His sight. The whole human race hath longed for this Day, that perchance it may fulfil that which well beseemeth its station, and is worthy of its destiny. Blessed is the man whom the affairs of the world have failed to deter from recognizing Him Who is the Lord of all things.

Bahá'u'lláh

6 Núr   10 June

THIS is the Day that God hath ordained to be a blessing unto the righteous, a retribution for the wicked, a bounty for the faithful and a fury of His wrath for the faithless and the froward. Verily He hath been made manifest, invested by God with invincible sovereignty. He hath revealed that wherewith naught on the earth or in the heavens can compare.

Bahá'u'lláh

7 Núr   11 June

INDEED all the Prophets have yearned to attain this Day. David saith: 'Who will bring me into the strong City?' By strong City is meant 'Akká. Its fortifications are very strong and this Wronged One is imprisoned within its walls. Likewise it is revealed in the Qur'án: 'Bring forth thy people from the darkness into the light and announce to them the days of God.' (14:5)

The glory with which this Day is invested hath been explicitly mentioned and clearly set forth in most heavenly Books and Scriptures. However, the divines of the age have debarred men from this transcendent station, and have kept them back from this Pinnacle of Glory, this Supreme Goal.

Bahá'u'lláh

8 Núr   12 June

GLORIFIED be God! All the heavenly Scriptures of the past attest to the greatness of this Day, the greatness of this Manifestation, the greatness of His signs, the greatness of His Word, the greatness of His constancy, the greatness of His pre-eminent station. Yet despite all this the people have remained heedless and are shut out as by a veil.

Bahá'u'lláh

9 Núr   13 June

THIS is the Day which the Pen of the Most High hath glorified in all the holy Scriptures. There is no verse in them that doth not declare the glory of His holy Name, and no Book that doth not testify unto the loftiness of this most exalted theme. Were We to make mention of all that hath been revealed in these heavenly Books and holy Scriptures concerning this Revelation, this Tablet would assume impossible dimensions.

Bahá'u'lláh

10 Núr   14 June

THIS is the King of Days, the Day that hath seen the coming of the Best-Beloved, Him Who through all eternity hath been acclaimed the Desire of the World. The world of being shineth in this Day with the resplendency of this Divine

Revelation. All created things extol its saving grace and sing its praises. The universe is wrapt in an ecstasy of joy and gladness. The Scriptures of past Dispensations celebrate the great jubilee that must needs greet this most Great Day of God. Well is it with him that hath lived to see this Day and hath recognized its station.

Bahá'u'lláh

11 Núr   15 June

SEIZE your chance inasmuch as a fleeting moment in this Day excelleth centuries of a bygone age . . . Neither sun nor moon hath witnessed a day such as this . . . It is evident that every age in which a Manifestation of God hath lived is divinely ordained and may, in a sense, be characterized as God's appointed Day. This Day, however, is unique and is to be distinguished from those that have preceded it. The designation 'Seal of Prophets' fully reveals and demonstrates its high station.

Bahá'u'lláh

12 Núr   16 June

SAY, this is the Day when the Speaker on Sinai hath mounted the throne of Revelation and the people have stood before the Lord of the worlds. This is the Day wherein the earth hath told out her tidings and hath laid bare her treasures; when the oceans have brought forth their pearls and the divine Lote-Tree its fruit; when the Sun hath shed its radiance and the Moons have diffused their lights, and the Heavens have revealed their stars, and the Hour its signs, and the Resurrection its dreadful majesty; when the pens

have unloosed their outpourings and the spirits have laid
bare their mysteries. Blessed is the man who recognizeth
Him and attaineth His presence, and woe betide such as
deny Him and turn aside from Him. I beseech God to aid
His servants to return unto Him. Verily He is the Pardoner,
the Forgiving, the Merciful.

Bahá'u'lláh

13 Núr   17 June

THE world is continually proclaiming these words: Beware, I
am evanescent, and so are all my outward appearances and
colours. Take ye heed of the changes and chances contrived
within me and be ye roused from your slumber. Nevertheless there is no discerning eye to see, nor is there a hearing
ear to hearken.

In this Day the inner ear exclaimeth and saith: Indeed well
is it with me, today is my day, inasmuch as the Voice of God
is calling aloud. And the essence of vision crieth out: Blessed
am I, this is my day, for the Ancient Beauty is shining
resplendent from the most exalted Horizon.

It behoveth the people of Bahá to invoke and entreat the
Lord of Names that perchance the people of the world may
not be deprived of the effusions of grace in His days.

Bahá'u'lláh

14 Núr   18 June

IN this Day a great festival is taking place in the Realm
above; for whatsoever was promised in the sacred Scriptures
hath been fulfilled. This is the Day of great rejoicing. It
behoveth everyone to hasten towards the court of His
nearness with exceeding joy, gladness, exultation and
delight and to deliver himself from the fire of remoteness.

O people of Tár! Through the strengthening power of My Name seize ye the chalice of knowledge, drink then your fill in defiance of the people of the world who have broken the Covenant of God and His Testament, rejected His proofs and clear tokens, and cavilled at His signs which have pervaded all that are in heaven and on earth.

Bahá'u'lláh

15 Núr   19 June

WHEN God sent forth His Prophet Muḥammad, on that day the termination of the prophetic cycle was foreordained in the knowledge of God. Yea, that promise hath indeed come true and the decree of God hath been accomplished as He hath ordained. Assuredly we are today living in the Days of God. These are the glorious days on the like of which the sun hath never risen in the past. These are the days which the people in bygone times eagerly expected. What hath then befallen you that ye are fast asleep? These are the days wherein God hath caused the Day-Star of Truth to shine resplendent. What hath then caused you to keep your silence? These are the appointed days which ye have been yearningly awaiting in the past – the days of the advent of divine justice. Render ye thanks unto God, O ye concourse of believers.

The Báb

16 Núr   20 June

VERILY I say, this is the Day in which mankind can behold the Face, and hear the Voice, of the Promised One. The Call of God hath been raised, and the light of His countenance hath been lifted up upon men. It behoveth every man to blot out the trace of every idle word from the tablet of his heart, and to gaze, with an open and unbiased mind, on the signs of His Revelation, the proofs of His Mission, and the tokens of His glory.

Great indeed is this Day! The allusions made to it in all the sacred Scriptures as the Day of God attest its greatness. The soul of every Prophet of God, of every Divine Messenger, hath thirsted for this wondrous Day.

Bahá'u'lláh

17 Núr   21 June

O THOU that hast fixed thine eyes upon My countenance! The Day Spring of Glory hath, in this Day, manifested its radiance, and the Voice of the Most High is calling. We have formerly uttered these words: 'This is not the day for any man to question his Lord. It behoveth whosoever hath hearkened to the Call of God, as voiced by Him Who is the Day Spring of Glory, to arise and cry out: "Here am I, here am I, O Lord of all Names; here am I, here am I, O Maker of the heavens! I testify that, through Thy Revelation, the things hidden in the Books of God have been revealed, and that whatsoever hath been recorded by Thy Messengers in the sacred Scriptures hath been fulfilled." '

Bahá'u'lláh

18 Núr   22 June

BY the righteousness of Mine own Self! Great, immeasurably great is this Cause! Mighty, inconceivably mighty is this Day! Blessed indeed is the man that hath forsaken all things, and fastened his eyes upon Him Whose face hath shed illumination upon all who are in the heavens and all who are on the earth.

Bahá'u'lláh

19 Núr   23 June

I TESTIFY, O my God, that this is the Day whereon Thy testimony hath been fulfilled, and Thy clear tokens have been manifested, and Thine utterances have been revealed, and Thy signs have been demonstrated, and the radiance of Thy countenance hath been diffused, and Thy proof hath been perfected, and Thine ascendancy hath been established, and Thy mercy hath overflowed, and the Day-Star of Thy grace hath shone forth with such brilliance that Thou didst manifest Him Who is the Revealer of Thyself and the Treasury of Thy wisdom and the Dawning-Place of Thy majesty and power. Thou didst establish His covenant with every one who hath been created in the kingdoms of earth and heaven and in the realms of revelation and of creation. Thou didst raise Him up to such heights that the wrongs inflicted by the oppressors have been powerless to deter Him from revealing Thy sovereignty, and the ascendancy of the wayward hath failed to prevent Him from demonstrating Thy power and from exalting Thy Cause.

Bahá'u'lláh

The month of Raḥmat begins at sunset.

6

Raḥmat
(Mercy)

Man's Response to the Covenant:
To Know and Recognize

Feast of Raḥmat

1 Raḥmat   24 June

KNOW thou that, according to what thy Lord, the Lord of all men, hath decreed in His Book, the favours vouchsafed by Him unto mankind have been, and will ever remain, limitless in their range. First and foremost among these favours, which the Almighty hath conferred upon man, is the gift of understanding. His purpose in conferring such a gift is none other except to enable His creature to know and recognize the one true God – exalted be His glory.

Bahá'u'lláh

2 Raḥmat   25 June

SAY: The first and foremost testimony establishing His truth is His own Self. Next to this testimony is His Revelation. For whoso faileth to recognize either the one or the other He hath established the words He hath revealed as proof of His reality and truth. This is, verily, an evidence of His tender mercy unto men. He hath endowed every soul with the capacity to recognize the signs of God. How could He, otherwise, have fulfilled His testimony unto men, if ye be of them that ponder His Cause in their hearts. He will never deal unjustly with any one, neither will He task a soul beyond its power. He, verily, is the Compassionate, the All-Merciful.

Bahá'u'lláh

3 Raḥmat   26 June

THE second Tajallí is to remain steadfast in the Cause of God – exalted be His glory – and to be unswerving in His love. And this can in no wise be attained except through full recognition of Him; and full recognition cannot be obtained save by faith in the blessed words: 'He doeth whatsoever He willeth.' Whoso tenaciously cleaveth unto this sublime word and drinketh deep from the living waters of utterance which are inherent therein, will be imbued with such a constancy that all the books of the world will be powerless to deter him from the Mother Book. O how glorious is this sublime station, this exalted rank, this ultimate purpose!

Bahá'u'lláh

4 Raḥmat   27 June

. . . every man hath been, and will continue to be, able of himself to appreciate the Beauty of God, the Glorified. Had he not been endowed with such a capacity, how could he be called to account for his failure? If, in the Day when all the peoples of the earth will be gathered together, any man should, whilst standing in the presence of God, be asked: 'Wherefore hast thou disbelieved in My Beauty and turned away from My Self', and if such a man should reply and say: 'Inasmuch as all men have erred, and none hath been found willing to turn his face to the Truth, I, too, following their example, have grievously failed to recognize the Beauty of the Eternal', such a plea will, assuredly, be rejected. For the faith of no man can be conditioned by any one except himself.

Bahá'u'lláh

5 Raḥmat   28 June

WE have chosen you out of the world to know and recognize Our Self. We have caused you to draw nigh unto the right side of Paradise – the Spot out of which the undying Fire crieth in manifold accents: 'There is none other God besides Me, the All-Powerful, the Most High!' Take heed lest ye allow yourselves to be shut out as by a veil from this Day Star that shineth above the day-spring of the Will of your Lord, the All-Merciful, and whose light hath encompassed both the small and the great. Purge your sight, that ye may perceive its glory with your own eyes, and depend not on the sight of any one except your self, for God hath never burdened any soul beyond its power. Thus hath it been sent down unto the Prophets and Messengers of old, and been recorded in all the Scriptures.

Bahá'u'lláh

6 Raḥmat   29 June

BLESSED is the man that hath acknowledged his belief in God and in His signs, and recognized that 'He shall not be asked of His doings'. Such a recognition hath been made by God the ornament of every belief, and its very foundation. Upon it must depend the acceptance of every goodly deed.

Fasten your eyes upon it, that haply the whisperings of the rebellious may not cause you to slip.

Bahá'u'lláh

7 Raḥmat   30 June

THE utter destitution into which this people have fallen doth surely suffice them, inasmuch as they have been deprived of the recognition of the essential Purpose and the knowledge of the Mystery and Substance of the Cause of God. For the highest and most excelling grace bestowed upon men is the grace of 'attaining unto the Presence of God' and of His recognition, which has been promised unto all people. This is the utmost degree of grace vouchsafed unto man by the All-Bountiful, the Ancient of Days, and the fullness of His absolute bounty upon His creatures.

Bahá'u'lláh

8 Raḥmat   1 July

ALL-PRAISE and glory be to God Who, through the power of His might, hath delivered His creation from the nakedness of non-existence, and clothed it with the mantle of life. From among all created things He hath singled out for His special favour the pure, the gem-like reality of man, and invested it with a unique capacity of knowing Him and of reflecting the greatness of His glory.

Bahá'u'lláh

9 Raḥmat   2 July

I BEAR witness, O my God, that Thou hast created me to know Thee and to worship Thee.

Bahá'u'lláh

10 Raḥmat   3 July

BY My Beauty! Nothing whatsoever shall, in this Day, be accepted from you, though ye continue to worship and prostrate yourselves before God throughout the eternity of His dominion. For all things are dependent upon His Will, and the worth of all acts is conditioned upon His acceptance and pleasure. The whole universe is but a handful of clay in His grasp. Unless one recognize God and love Him, his cry shall not be heard by God in this Day. This is of the essence of His Faith, did ye but know it.

Bahá'u'lláh

11 Raḥmat   4 July

FOR every one of you his paramount duty is to choose for himself that on which no other may infringe and none usurp from him. Such a thing – and to this the Almighty is My witness – is the love of God, could ye but perceive it.

Bahá'u'lláh

12 Raḥmat   5 July

O SON OF BEING!
Love Me, that I may love thee. If thou lovest Me not, My love can in no wise reach thee. Know this, O servant.

Bahá'u'lláh

13 Raḥmat   6 July

HAVING created the world and all that liveth and moveth

therein, He, through the direct operation of His uncon-strained and sovereign Will, chose to confer upon man the unique distinction and capacity to know Him and to love Him – a capacity that must needs be regarded as the generating impulse and the primary purpose underlying the whole of creation.

Bahá'u'lláh

14 Raḥmat 7 July

THE first duty prescribed by God for His servants is the recognition of Him Who is the Day Spring of His Revelation and the Fountain of His laws, Who representeth the Godhead in both the Kingdom of His Cause and the world of creation. Whoso achieveth this duty hath attained unto all good . . . It behoveth every one who reacheth this most sublime station, this summit of transcendent glory, to observe every ordinance of Him Who is the Desire of the world. These twin duties are inseparable. Neither is accept-able without the other.

Bahá'u'lláh

15 Raḥmat 8 July

THE beginning of all things is the knowledge of God, and the end of all things is strict observance of whatsoever hath been sent down from the empyrean of the Divine Will that pervadeth all that is in the heavens and all that is on the earth.

Bahá'u'lláh

The commemoration of the Martyrdom of the Báb begins at sunset.

Martyrdom of the Báb

16 Raḥmat   *9 July*

THE supreme cause for creating the world and all that is
therein is for man to know God. In this Day whosoever is
guided by the fragrance of the raiment of His mercy to gain
admittance into the pristine Abode, which is the station of
recognizing the Source of divine commandments and the
Dayspring of His Revelation, hath everlastingly attained
unto all good. Having reached this lofty station a twofold
obligation resteth upon every soul. One is to be steadfast in
the Cause with such steadfastness that were all the peoples
of the world to attempt to prevent him from turning to the
Source of Revelation, they would be powerless to do so.
The other is observance of the divine ordinances which
have streamed forth from the wellspring of His heavenly-
propelled Pen. For man's knowledge of God cannot develop
fully and adequately save by observing whatsoever hath
been ordained by Him and is set forth in His heavenly Book.

Bahá'u'lláh

The anniversary of the Martyrdom of the Báb is observed at noon.

17 Raḥmat   *10 July*

THE ordinances of God have been sent down from the
heaven of His most august Revelation. All must diligently
observe them. Man's supreme distinction, his real advancement, his final victory, have always depended, and will
continue to depend, upon them. Whoso keepeth the
commandments of God shall attain everlasting felicity.

Bahá'u'lláh

18 Raḥmat   11 July

SAY: From My laws the sweet smelling savour of My garment can be smelled, and by their aid the standards of victory will be planted upon the highest peaks. The Tongue of My power hath, from the heaven of My omnipotent glory, addressed to My creation these words: 'Observe My commandments, for the love of My beauty.' Happy is the lover that hath inhaled the divine fragrance of his Best-Beloved from these words, laden with the perfume of a grace which no tongue can describe. By My life! He who hath drunk the choice wine of fairness from the hands of My bountiful favour, will circle around My commandments that shine above the Day Spring of My creation.

Bahá'u'lláh

19 Raḥmat   12 July

WHENEVER My laws appear like the sun in the heaven of Mine utterance, they must be faithfully obeyed by all, though My decree be such as to cause the heaven of every religion to be cleft asunder. He doeth what He pleaseth. He chooseth; and none may question His choice. Whatsoever He, the Well-Beloved, ordaineth, the same is, verily, beloved. To this He Who is the Lord of all creation beareth Me witness. Whoso hath inhaled the sweet fragrance of the All-Merciful, and recognized the Source of this utterance, will welcome with his own eyes the shafts of the enemy, that he may establish the truth of the laws of God amongst men. Well is it with him that hath turned thereunto, and apprehended the meaning of His decisive decree.

Bahá'u'lláh

The month of Kalimát begins at sunset.

7

Kalimát
(Words)

The Lesser Covenant:
The Appointment of 'Abdu'l-Bahá

Feast of Kalimát

1 Kalimát — *13 July*

THERE hath branched from the Sadratu'l-Muntahá this sacred and glorious Being, this Branch of Holiness; well is it with him that hath sought His shelter and abideth beneath His shadow. Verily the Limb of the Law of God hath sprung forth from this Root which God hath firmly implanted in the Ground of His Will, and Whose Branch hath been so uplifted as to encompass the whole of creation. Magnified be He, therefore, for this sublime, this blessed, this mighty, this exalted Handiwork!

Bahá'u'lláh

2 Kalimát — *14 July*

THE Will of the divine Testator is this: It is incumbent upon the Aghsán, the Afnán and My kindred to turn, one and all, their faces towards the Most Mighty Branch. Consider that which We have revealed in Our Most Holy Book: 'When the ocean of My presence hath ebbed and the Book of My Revelation is ended, turn your faces toward Him Whom God

75

hath purposed, Who hath branched from this Ancient Root.' The object of this sacred verse is none other except the Most Mighty Branch ['Abdu'l-Bahá]. Thus have We graciously revealed unto you our potent Will, and I am verily the Gracious, the All-Powerful. Verily God hath ordained the station of the Greater Branch [Muḥammad-'Alí] to be beneath that of the Most Great Branch ['Abdu'l-Bahá]. He is in truth the Ordainer, the All-Wise. We have chosen 'the Greater' after 'the Most Great', as decreed by Him Who is the All-Knowing, the All Informed.

Bahá'u'lláh

3 Kalimát   15 July

WHOSO turneth towards Him hath turned towards God, and whoso turneth away from Him hath turned away from My Beauty, hath repudiated My Proof, and transgressed against Me. He is the Trust of God amongst you, His charge within you, His manifestation unto you and His appearance among His favoured servants . . . We have sent Him down in the form of a human temple. Blest and sanctified be God Who createth whatsoever He willeth through His inviolable, His infallible decree. They who deprive themselves of the shadow of the Branch are lost in the wilderness of error, are consumed by the heat of worldly desires, and are of those who will assuredly perish.

Bahá'u'lláh

4 Kalimát   16 July

A WORD hath, as a token of Our grace, gone forth from the Most Great Tablet – a Word which God hath adorned with

the ornament of His own Self, and made it sovereign over
the earth and all that is therein, and a sign of His greatness
and power among its people . . . Render thanks unto God,
O people, for His appearance; for verily He is the most great
Favour unto you, the most perfect bounty upon you; and
through Him every mouldering bone is quickened.

Bahá'u'lláh

5 Kalimát   17 July

WHEN the Mystic Dove will have winged its flight from its
Sanctuary of Praise and sought its far-off goal, its hidden
habitation, refer ye whatsoever ye understand not in the
Book to Him Who hath branched from this mighty Stock.

Bahá'u'lláh

6 Kalimát   18 July

O THOU My Greatest Branch! . . . Verily, we have ordained
Thee the Guardian of all the creatures, and a Protection to
all those in the heavens and earth, and a Fortress to those
who believe in God, the One, the Omniscient! . . . I beg of
Him to water the earth and all that is in it by Thee . . .

Bahá'u'lláh

7 Kalimát   19 July

I AM according to the explicit texts of the *Kitáb-i-Aqdas* and
the *Kitáb-i-'Ahd* the manifest Interpreter of the Word of

God . . . Whoso deviates from my interpretation is a victim of his own fancy.

'Abdu'l-Bahá

8 Kalimát   20 July

IN the Book of Aqdas, He has given positive command in two clear instances and has explicitly appointed the Interpreter of the Book. Also in all the Divine Tablets, especially in the Chapter of The Branch – all the meanings of which mean the Servitude of 'Abdu'l-Bahá, that is 'Abdu'l-Bahá – all that was needed to explain the Centre of the Covenant and the Interpreter of the Book has been revealed from the Supreme Pen. Now as 'Abdu'l-Bahá is the Interpreter of the Book He says that the 'Chapter of The Branch' means 'Abdu'l-Bahá, that is, the Servitude of 'Abdu'l-Bahá, and none other.

'Abdu'l-Bahá

9 Kalimát   21 July

INASMUCH as great differences and divergences of denominational belief had arisen throughout the past, every man with a new idea attributing it to God, Bahá'u'lláh desired that there should not be any ground or reason for disagreement among the Bahá'ís. Therefore, with His own pen He wrote the Book of His Covenant, addressing His relations and all people of the world, saying, 'Verily, I have appointed One Who is the Centre of My Covenant. All must obey Him; all must turn to Him; He is the Expounder of My Book, and He is informed of My purpose. All must turn to Him. Whatsoever He says is correct, for, verily, He knoweth the texts of My Book. Other than He, no one doth know My Book.' The purpose of this statement is that there should never be discord and divergence among the Bahá'ís but that they should always be unified and agreed.

'Abdu'l-Bahá

10 *Kalimát* 22 July

IN His prayers Bahá'ulláh also said, 'O God! Whosoever violates My Covenant, O God, humiliate him. Verily, whosoever violates My Covenant, O God, erase and efface him.' In all His Tablets, among which is the Tablet of the Branch, He has mentioned and explained the attributes and qualities of the Personage to Whom He referred in the Book of His Covenant. He has fully expounded the function and potency of that Personage, so that no one shall say, 'I understand this from the writings of Bahá'u'lláh', for He has appointed the Centre, or Expounder, of the Book. He said, 'Verily, He is the appointed one; other than He, there is none', intending that no sects or prejudices should be formed, and preventing every man here and there with a new thought from creating dissension and variance.

'Abdu'l-Bahá

11 *Kalimát* 23 July

INASMUCH as there was no appointed explainer of the Book of Christ, everyone made the claim to authority, saying, 'This is the true pathway and others are not.' To ward off such dissensions as these and prevent any person from creating a division or sect the Blessed Perfection, Bahá'u'lláh, appointed a central authoritative Personage, declaring Him to be the expounder of the Book. This implies that the people in general do not understand the meanings of the Book, but this appointed One does understand. Therefore, Bahá'u'lláh said, 'He is the explainer of My Book and the Centre of My Testament.' In the last verses of the Book instructions are revealed, declaring that, 'After Me', you must turn toward a special Personage and 'whatsoever He says is correct'. In the Book of the Covenant Bahá'u'lláh declares that by these two verses this Personage is meant.

'Abdu'l-Bahá

12 Kalimát   24 July

AFTER the departure of Christ various sects and denominations arose, each one claiming to be the true channel of Christianity, but none of them possessed a written authority from Christ; none could produce proof from Him; yet all claimed His sanction and approval. Bahá'u'lláh has written a Covenant and Testament with His own pen, declaring that the One Whom He has appointed the Centre of the Covenant shall be turned to and obeyed by all.

'Abdu'l-Bahá

13 Kalimát   25 July

IN accordance with the explicit text of the *Kitáb-i-Aqdas* Bahá'u'lláh hath made the Centre of the Covenant the Interpreter of His Word – a Covenant so firm and mighty that from the beginning of time until the present day no religious Dispensation hath produced its like.

'Abdu'l-Bahá

14 Kalimát   26 July

'ALL must turn to Him. Whatsoever He says is correct, for, verily, He knoweth the texts of My Book. Other than He, no one doth know My Book.' The purpose of this statement is that there should never be discord and divergence among the Bahá'ís but that they should always be unified and agreed . . . Therefore, whosoever obeys the Centre of the Covenant appointed by Bahá'u'lláh has obeyed Bahá'u'lláh, and whosoever disobeys Him has disobeyed Bahá'u'lláh . . . Beware! Beware! lest any one should speak from the authority of his own thoughts or create a new thing out of himself . . . Bahá'u'lláh shuns such souls.

'Abdu'l-Bahá

15 Kalimát   27 July

ANY opinion expressed by the Centre of the Covenant is correct, and there is no reason for disobedience by anyone. Be watchful, for perchance there may be violators of the Covenant among you. Do not listen to them. Read the Book of the Covenant. All have been commanded to obey the Covenant, and the first admonition is addressed to the sons of Bahá'u'lláh, the Branches: 'You must turn to the appointed Centre; He is the expounder of the Book.'

'Abdu'l-Bahá

16 Kalimát   28 July

BAHÁ'U'LLÁH covenanted, not that I am the Promised One, but that 'Abdu'l-Bahá is the Expounder of the Book and the Centre of His Covenant, and that the Promised One of

Bahá'u'lláh will appear after one thousand or thousands of years. This is the Covenant which Bahá'u'lláh made. If a person deviates, he is not acceptable at the threshold of Bahá'u'lláh. In case of differences, 'Abdu'l-Bahá must be consulted. All must revolve around his good pleasure. After 'Abdu'l-Bahá, whenever the Universal House of Justice is organized it will ward off differences.

'Abdu'l-Bahá

17 Kalimát   29 July

BAHÁ'U'LLÁH made a covenant concerning a promised One who will become manifest after one thousand or thousands of years. He likewise, with His Supreme Pen, entered into a great Covenant and Testament with all the Bahá'ís whereby they were all commanded to follow the Centre of the Covenant after His departure, and turn not away even to a hair's breadth from obeying Him.

'Abdu'l-Bahá

18 Kalimát   30 July

BUT in this Blessed Dispensation, for the sake of the permanency of the Cause of God and the avoidance of dissension amongst the people of God, the Blessed Beauty (may my soul be a sacrifice unto Him), has through the Supreme Pen written the Covenant and the Testament; He appointed a Centre, the Exponent of the Book and the annuller of disputes. Whatever is written or said by Him is conformable to the truth and under the protection of the Blessed Beauty. He is infallible. The express purpose of this last Will and Testament is to set aside disputes from the world.

'Abdu'l-Bahá

19 Kalimát   *31 July*

. . . there are some who for the sake of personal interest and prestige will attempt to sow the seeds of sedition and disloyalty among you. To protect and safeguard the religion of God from this and all other attack, the Centre of the Covenant has been named and appointed by Bahá'u'lláh.

'Abdu'l-Bahá

The month of Kamál begins at sunset.

8

Kamál
(Perfection)

The Centre of the Covenant:
The Station of 'Abdu'l-Bahá

Feast of Kamál

1 Kamál   1 August

MY name is 'Abdu'l-Bahá. My qualification is 'Abdu'l-Bahá.
My reality is 'Abdu'l-Bahá. My praise is 'Abdu'l-Bahá.
Thraldom to the Blessed Perfection is my glorious and
refulgent diadem, and servitude to all the human race my
perpetual religion . . . No name, no title, no mention, no
commendation have I, nor will ever have, except 'Abdu'l-
Bahá. This is my longing. This is my greatest yearning. This
is my eternal life. This is my everlasting glory.

'Abdu'l-Bahá

2 Kamál   2 August

'ABDU'L-BAHÁ is Himself a servant at the Threshold of the
Blessed Beauty and a manifestation of pure and utter
servitude at the Threshold of the Almighty. He hath no
other station or title, no other rank or power. This is my
ultimate Purpose, my eternal Paradise, my holiest Temple
and my Sadratu'l-Muntahá.

'Abdu'l-Bahá

3 Kamál   3 August

THIS is my firm, my unshakable conviction, the essence of
my unconcealed and explicit belief – a conviction and belief
which the denizens of the Abhá Kingdom fully share: The
Blessed Beauty is the Sun of Truth, and His light the light of
truth. The Báb is likewise the Sun of Truth, and His light the
light of truth . . . My station is the station of servitude – a
servitude which is complete, pure and real, firmly established, enduring, obvious, explicitly revealed and subject to
no interpretation whatever . . . I am the Interpreter of the
Word of God; such is my interpretation.

'Abdu'l-Bahá

4 Kamál   4 August

I AFFIRM that the true meaning, the real significance, the
innermost secret of these verses, of these very words, is my
own servitude to the sacred Threshold of the Abhá Beauty,
my complete self-effacement, my utter nothingness before
Him. This is my resplendent crown, my most precious
adorning. On this I pride myself in the kingdom of earth and
heaven. Therein I glory among the company of the well-
favoured! No one is permitted to give these verses any other
interpretation.

'Abdu'l-Bahá

5 Kamál   5 August

WE have made Thee a shelter for all mankind, a shield unto
all who are in heaven and on earth, a stronghold for
whosoever hath believed in God, the Incomparable, the

All-Knowing. God grant that through Thee He may protect them, may enrich and sustain them, that He may inspire Thee with that which shall be a well-spring of wealth unto all created things, an ocean of bounty unto all men, and the dayspring of mercy unto all peoples.

Bahá'u'lláh

6 Kamál   6 August

THE glory of God rest upon Thee and upon whosoever serveth Thee and circleth around Thee. Woe, great woe, betide him that opposeth and injureth Thee. Well is it with him that sweareth fealty to Thee; the fire of hell torment him who is Thine enemy.

Bahá'u'lláh

7 Kamál   7 August

O THOU Who art the apple of Mine eye! My glory, the ocean of My loving-kindness, the sun of My bounty, the heaven of My mercy rest upon Thee. We pray God to illumine the world through Thy knowledge and wisdom, to ordain for Thee that which will gladden Thine heart and impart consolation to Thine eyes.

Bahá'u'lláh

8 Kamál   8 August

PRAISE be to Him Who hath honoured the Land of Bá through the presence of Him round Whom all names

89

revolve. All the atoms of the earth have announced unto all created things that from behind the gate of the Prison-city there hath appeared and above its horizon there hath shone the Orb of the beauty of the great, the Most Mighty Branch of God – His ancient and immutable Mystery – proceeding on its way to another land. Sorrow, thereby, hath enveloped the Prison-city, whilst another land rejoiceth.

Bahá'u'lláh

9 Kamál   9 August

BLESSED, doubly blessed, is the ground which His footsteps have trodden, the eye that hath been cheered by the beauty of His countenance, the ear that hath been honoured by hearkening to His call, the heart that hath tasted the sweetness of His love, the breast that hath dilated through His remembrance, the pen that hath voiced His praise, the scroll that hath borne the testimony of His writings. We beseech God – blessed and exalted be He – that He may honour us with meeting Him soon. He is, in truth, the All-Hearing, the All-Powerful, He Who is ready to answer.

Bahá'u'lláh

10 Kamál   10 August

O GREATEST Branch! Verily, Thy illness caused Me sorrow, but God will cure Thee, and He is the most generous and best helper. Glory be upon Thee and upon those who serve Thee and encircle Thee! Woe and torment be upon him who opposes and torments Thee! Blessed is he who befriends Thee, and hell be for him who opposes Thee!

Bahá'u'lláh

11 Kamál   11 August

THE force of the utterance of the Most Great Branch and His powers are not as yet fully revealed. In the future it will be seen how He, alone and unaided, shall raise the banner of the Most Great Name in the midmost heart of the world, with power and authority and Divine effulgence. It will be seen how He shall gather together the peoples of the earth under the tent of peace and concord.

Bahá'u'lláh

12 Kamál   12 August

O THOU who posed a test for 'Abdu'l-Bahá! Is it seemly for a man like thee to test a servant submissive and lowly before God? Nay by God, it is given to the Centre of the Covenant to test the peoples of the world.

'Abdu'l-Bahá

13 Kamál   13 August

THESE Spiritual Assemblies are aided by the Spirit of God. Their defender is 'Abdu'l-Bahá. Over them He spreadeth His wings. What bounty is there greater than this?

'Abdu'l-Bahá

14 Kamál   14 August

ANOTHER commandment I give unto you, that ye love one another even as I love you . . . look at one another with the eye of perfection; look at Me, follow Me, be as I am; take no thought for yourselves or your lives, whether ye eat or whether ye sleep, whether ye are comfortable, whether ye are well or ill, whether ye are with friends or foes, whether ye receive praise or blame . . . Look at Me and be as I am; ye must die to yourselves and to the world, so shall ye be born again and enter the Kingdom of Heaven. Behold a candle how it gives its light. It weeps its life away drop by drop in order to give forth its flame of light.

'Abdu'l-Bahá

15 Kamál   15 August

THOU knowest, O my God, that I desire for Him naught except that which Thou didst desire, and have chosen Him for no purpose save that which Thou hadst intended for Him. Render Him victorious, therefore, through Thy hosts of earth and heaven . . . Ordain, I beseech Thee, by the ardour of My love for Thee and My yearning to manifest Thy Cause, for Him, as well as for them that love Him, that which Thou hast destined for Thy Messengers and the Trustees of Thy Revelation. Verily, Thou art the Almighty, the All-Powerful.

Bahá'u'lláh

16 Kamál   16 August

O GOD! This is a Branch which has sprung forth from the Tree of Oneness, the Sadrat of Thy Unity. O God! Thou seest Him looking to Thee and clinging to the rope of Thy

Bounties. Protect Him in the shelter of Thy Mercy! Thou knowest, O My God, that I do not desire Him save for what Thou dost desire Him, and I do not choose Him save for what Thou dost choose Him. Assist Him with the Hosts of Thy earth and Thy heaven. Assist, O God, those who assist Him, and choose those who choose Him. Confirm those who draw nigh unto Him, and debase those who deny Him and do not want Him.

Bahá'u'lláh

17 Kamál   17 August

O GOD, my God! Thou seest this wronged servant of Thine, held fast in the talons of ferocious lions, of ravening wolves, of bloodthirsty beasts. Graciously assist me, through my love for Thee, that I may drink deep of the chalice that brimmeth over with faithfulness to Thee and is filled with Thy bountiful Grace; so that, fallen upon the dust, I may sink prostrate and senseless whilst my vesture is dyed crimson with my blood. This is my wish, my heart's desire, my hope, my pride, my glory. Grant, O Lord my God, and my Refuge, that in my last hour, my end, may even as musk shed its fragrance of glory! Is there a bounty greater than this? Nay, by Thy Glory! I call Thee to witness that no day passeth but that I quaff my fill from this cup, so grievous are the misdeeds wrought by them that have broken the Covenant, kindled discord, showed their malice, stirred sedition in the land, and dishonoured Thee amidst Thy servants. Lord! Shield Thou from these Covenant-breakers the mighty Stronghold of Thy Faith and protect Thy secret Sanctuary from the onslaught of the ungodly. Thou art in truth the Mighty, the Powerful, the Gracious, the Strong.

'Abdu'l-Bahá

18 Kamál   18 August

HE IS GOD!

O my Lord, my heart's Desire, Thou Whom I ever invoke, Thou Who art my Aider and my Shelter, my Helper and my Refuge! Thou seest me submerged in an ocean of calamities that overwhelm the soul, of afflictions that oppress the heart, of woes that disperse Thy gathering, of ills and pains that scatter Thy flock. Sore trials have compassed me round and perils have from all sides beset me. Thou seest me immersed in a sea of unsurpassed tribulation, sunk into a fathomless abyss, afflicted by mine enemies, and consumed with the flame of their hate, enkindled by my kinsmen with whom Thou didst make Thy strong Covenant and Thy firm Testament, wherein Thou biddest them turn their hearts to this wronged one, to keep away from me the foolish, the unjust, and refer unto this lonely one all that about which they differ in Thy Holy Book, so that the Truth may be revealed unto them, their doubts may be dispelled and Thy manifest Signs be spread abroad.

'Abdu'l-Bahá

19 Kamál   19 August

BY God, O people, My eye weeps, and the eye of 'Alí weeps in the Supreme Concourse; My heart throbs, and the heart of Muḥammad throbs in the Courts of Abhá; My heart and the hearts of the Prophets lament with the people of knowledge, if you are those who are possessed of sight. My sorrow is not for Myself, but for the One Who comes after Me in the Shadow of the Cause with a clear, undeniable reign; because these will not acknowledge His Manifestation and will deny His evidences and verses, will dispute His

power, will antagonize Him and will be traitors to His Cause
– as they did to His Person in those days – and ye were
witnesses.

Bahá'u'lláh

The month of Asmá' begins at sunset.

9

Asmá'
(Names)

*Institutions of the Covenant:
The Guardianship and the
Universal House of Justice*

Feast of Asmá'

1 Asmá'   *20 August*

SALUTATION and praise, blessing and glory rest upon that primal branch of the Divine and Sacred Lote-Tree, grown out, blest, tender, verdant, and flourishing from the Twin Holy Trees; the most wondrous, unique, and priceless pearl that doth gleam from out the Twin surging seas; upon the offshoots of the Tree of Holiness, the twigs of the Celestial Tree, they that in the Day of the Great Dividing have stood fast and firm in the Covenant; upon the Hands (pillars) of the Cause of God that have diffused widely the Divine Fragrances, declared His Proofs, proclaimed His Faith, published abroad His Law, detached themselves from all things but Him, stood for righteousness in this world, and kindled the Fire of the Love of God in the very hearts and souls of His servants; upon them that have believed, rested assured, stood steadfast in His Covenant, and followed the Light that after my passing shineth from the Dayspring of Divine Guidance – for behold! he is the blest and sacred bough that hath branched out from the Twin Holy Trees. Well is it with him that seeketh the shelter of his shade that shadoweth all mankind.

'Abdu'l-Bahá

99

2 Asmá'   21 August

O MY loving friends! After the passing away of this wronged one, it is incumbent upon the Aghsán (Branches), the Afnán (Twigs) of the Sacred Lote-Tree, the Hands (pillars) of the Cause of God, and the loved ones of the Abhá Beauty to turn unto Shoghi Effendi – the youthful branch branched from the Two hallowed and sacred Lote-Trees and the fruit grown from the union of the Two offshoots of the Tree of Holiness – as he is the sign of God, the chosen branch, the guardian of the Cause of God, he unto whom all the Aghsán, the Afnán, the Hands of the Cause of God, and His loved ones must turn. He is the expounder of the words of God and after him will succeed the first-born of his lineal descendants.

'Abdu'l-Bahá

3 Asmá'   22 August

O YE, the faithful loved ones of 'Abdu'l-Bahá! It is incumbent upon you to take the greatest care of Shoghi Effendi, the twig that hath branched from and the fruit given forth by the Two hallowed and Divine Lote-Trees, that no dust of despondency and sorrow may stain his radiant nature, that day by day he may wax greater in happiness, in joy and spirituality, and may grow to become even as a fruitful tree.

For he is, after 'Abdu'l-Bahá, the guardian of the Cause of God, the Afnán, the Hands (pillars) of the Cause and the beloved of the Lord must obey him and turn unto him. He that obeyeth him not, hath not obeyed God; he that turneth away from him, hath turned away from God; and he that denieth him, hath denied the True One. Beware lest anyone falsely interpret these words, and like unto them that have broken the Covenant after the Day of Ascension (of

Bahá'u'lláh) advance a pretext, raise the standard of revolt, wax stubborn, and open wide the door of false interpretation. To none is given the right to put forth his own opinion or express his particular convictions. All must seek guidance and turn unto the Centre of the Cause and the House of Justice. And he that turneth unto whatsoever else is indeed in grievous error.

The Glory of Glories rest upon you!

'Abdu'l-Bahá

4 Asmá'   23 August

THE sacred and youthful branch, the guardian of the Cause of God as well as the Universal House of Justice, to be universally elected and established, are both under the care and protection of the Abhá Beauty, under the shelter and unerring guidance of His Holiness, the Exalted One (may my life be offered up for them both). Whatsoever they decide is of God. Whoso obeyeth him not, neither obeyeth them, hath not obeyed God; whoso rebelleth against him and against them hath rebelled against God; whoso opposeth him hath opposed God; whoso contendeth with them hath contended with God; whoso disputeth with him hath disputed with God; whoso denieth him hath denied God; whoso disbelieveth in him hath disbelieved in God; whoso deviateth, separateth himself, and turneth aside from him hath in truth deviated, separated himself, and turned aside from God. May the wrath, the fierce indignation, the vengeance of God rest upon him!

'Abdu'l-Bahá

5 Asmá'   24 August

AND now, concerning the House of Justice which God hath

ordained as the source of all good and freed from all error, it must be elected by universal suffrage, that is, by the believers. Its members must be manifestations of the fear of God and day-springs of knowledge and understanding, must be steadfast in God's faith and the well-wishers of all mankind. By this House is meant the Universal House of Justice, that is, in all countries, a secondary House of Justice must be instituted, and these secondary Houses of Justice must elect the members of the Universal one. Unto this body all things must be referred. It enacteth all ordinances and regulations that are not to be found in the explicit Holy Text. By this body all the difficult problems are to be resolved and the guardian of the Cause of God is its sacred head and the distinguished member for life of that body. Should he not attend in person its deliberations, he must appoint one to represent him. Should any of the members commit a sin, injurious to the common weal, the guardian of the Cause of God hath at his own discretion the right to expel him, whereupon the people must elect another one in his stead. This House of Justice enacteth the laws and the government enforceth them. The legislative body must reinforce the executive, the executive must aid and assist the legislative body so that through the close union and harmony of these two forces, the foundation of fairness and justice may become firm and strong, that all the regions of the world may become as Paradise itself.

'Abdu'l-Bahá

6 Asmá'   25 August

HE has ordained and established the House of Justice, which is endowed with a political as well as a religious function, the consummate union and blending of church and state. This institution is under the protecting power of Bahá'u'lláh Himself. A universal, or international, House of Justice shall also be organized. Its rulings shall be in accordance with the commands and teachings of Bahá'u'lláh, and that which the Universal House of Justice ordains shall be obeyed by all mankind. This international House of Justice shall be appointed and organized from the Houses of Justice of the whole world, and all the world shall come under its administration.

'Abdu'l-Bahá

7 Asmá'   26 August

THE Supreme House of Justice should be elected according to the system followed in the election of the Parliaments of Europe. And when the countries would be guided the Houses of Justice of the various countries would elect the Supreme House of Justice.

At whatever time all the beloved of God in each country appoint their delegates, and these in turn elect their representatives, and these representatives elect a body, that body shall be regarded as the Supreme House of Justice.

'Abdu'l-Bahá

8 Asmá'   27 August

ACCORDING to the fundamental laws which We have formerly revealed in the Kitáb-i-Aqdas and other Tablets, all affairs are committed to the care of just kings and presidents and of the Trustees of the House of Justice. Having pondered on that which We have enunciated, every man of equity and discernment will readily perceive, with his inner and outer eyes, the splendours of the day-star of justice which radiate therefrom.

Bahá'u'lláh

9 Asmá' 28 August

THIS passage, now written by the Pen of Glory, is accounted as part of the Most Holy Book: The men of God's House of Justice have been charged with the affairs of the people. They, in truth, are the Trustees of God among His servants and the daysprings of authority in His countries.

Bahá'u'lláh

10 Asmá' 29 August

IT is incumbent upon these members (of the Universal House of Justice) to gather in a certain place and deliberate upon all problems which have caused difference, questions that are obscure, and matters that are not expressly recorded in the Book. Whatsoever they decide has the same effect as the Text itself. And inasmuch as this House of Justice hath power to enact laws that are not expressly recorded in the Book and bear upon daily transactions, so also it hath power to repeal the same. Thus for example, the House of Justice enacteth today a certain law and enforceth it, and a hundred years hence, circumstances having profoundly changed and the conditions having altered, another House of Justice will then have power, according to the exigencies of the time, to alter that law. This it can do because that law formeth no part of the Divine Explicit Text. The House of Justice is both the Initiator and the Abrogator of its own laws.

'Abdu'l-Bahá

11 Asmá'   30 August

IT is incumbent upon the Trustees of the House of Justice to take counsel together regarding those things which have not outwardly been revealed in the Book, and to enforce that which is agreeable to them. God will verily inspire them with whatsoever He willeth, and He, verily, is the Provider, the Omniscient.

Bahá'u'lláh

12 Asmá'   31 August

THOSE matters of major importance which constitute the foundation of the Law of God are explicitly recorded in the Text, but subsidiary laws are left to the House of Justice. The wisdom of this is that the times never remain the same, for change is a necessary quality and an essential attribute of this world, and of time and place. Therefore the House of Justice will take action accordingly.

'Abdu'l-Bahá

13 Asmá'   1 September

INASMUCH as for each day there is a new problem and for every problem an expedient solution, such affairs should be referred to the House of Justice that the members thereof may act according to the needs and requirements of the time. They that, for the sake of God, arise to serve His Cause, are the recipients of divine inspiration from the unseen Kingdom. It is incumbent upon all to be obedient unto them. All matters of State should be referred to the

House of Justice, but acts of worship must be observed according to that which God hath revealed in His Book.

Bahá'u'lláh

14 Asmá'   2 September

LET it not be imagined that the House of Justice will take any decision according to its own concepts and opinions. God forbid! The Supreme House of Justice will take decisions and establish laws through the inspiration and confirmation of the Holy Spirit, because it is in the safekeeping and under the shelter and protection of the Ancient Beauty, and obedience to its decisions is a bounden and essential duty and an absolute obligation, and there is no escape for anyone.

'Abdu'l-Bahá

15 Asmá'   3 September

SAY, O People: Verily the Supreme House of Justice is under the wings of your Lord, the Compassionate, the All-Merciful, that is under His protection, His care, and His shelter, for He has commanded the firm believers to obey that blessed, sanctified, and all-subduing body, whose sovereignty is divinely ordained and of the Kingdom of Heaven and whose laws are inspired and spiritual.

'Abdu'l-Bahá

16 Asmá'   4 September

BRIEFLY, this is the wisdom of referring the laws of society to the House of Justice. In the religion of Islám . . . not every ordinance was explicitly revealed; nay not a tenth part of a tenth part was included in the Text; although all matters of major importance were specifically referred to, there were undoubtedly thousands of laws which were unspecified. These were devised by the divines of a later age according to the laws of Islamic jurisprudence, and individual divines made conflicting deductions from the original revealed ordinances. All these were enforced. Today this process of deduction is the right of the body of the House of Justice, and the deductions and conclusions of individual learned men have no authority, unless they are endorsed by the House of Justice. The difference is precisely this, that from the conclusions and endorsements of the body of the House of Justice whose members are elected by and known to the worldwide Bahá'í community, no differences will arise; whereas the conclusions of individual divines and scholars would definitely lead to differences, and result in schism, division, and dispersion. The oneness of the Word would be destroyed, the unity of the Faith would disappear, and the edifice of the Faith of God would be shaken.

'Abdu'l-Bahá

17 Asmá'   5 September

IT is incumbent upon the men of God's House of Justice to fix their gaze by day and by night upon that which hath shone forth from the Pen of Glory for the training of peoples, the upbuilding of nations, the protection of man and the safeguarding of his honour.

Bahá'u'lláh

18 Asmá'   6 September

WE exhort the men of the House of Justice and command them to ensure the protection and safeguarding of men, women and children. It is incumbent upon them to have the utmost regard for the interests of the people at all times and under all conditions. Blessed is the ruler who succoureth the captive, and the rich one who careth for the poor, and the just one who secureth from the wrong doer the rights of the downtrodden, and happy the trustee who observeth that which the Ordainer, the Ancient of Days hath prescribed unto him.

Bahá'u'lláh

19 Asmá'   7 September

IT is incumbent upon the ministers of the House of Justice to promote the Lesser Peace so that the people of the earth may be relieved from the burden of exorbitant expenditures. This matter is imperative and absolutely essential, inasmuch as hostilities and conflict lie at the root of affliction and calamity.

Bahá'u'lláh

The month of 'Izzat begins at sunset.

10

'Izzat
(Might)

The Eternal Covenant

Feast of 'Izzat

1 'Izzat   *8 September*

WHOSO layeth claim to a Revelation direct from God, ere
the expiration of a full thousand years, such a man is
assuredly a lying impostor. We pray God that He may
graciously assist him to retract and repudiate such claim.
Should he repent, God will, no doubt, forgive him. If,
however, he persisteth in his error, God will, assuredly, send
down one who will deal mercilessly with him. Terrible,
indeed, is God in punishing! Whosoever interpreteth this
verse otherwise than its obvious meaning is deprived of the
Spirit of God and of His mercy which encompasseth all
created things. Fear God, and follow not your idle fancies.
Nay, rather follow the bidding of your Lord, the Almighty,
the All-Wise.

Bahá'u'lláh

2 'Izzat   *9 September*

SHOULD a man appear ere the lapse of a full thousand years –
each year consisting of twelve months according to the

111

Qur'án, and of nineteen months of nineteen days each, according to the Bayán – and if such a man reveal to your eyes all the signs of God, unhesitatingly reject him!

Bahá'u'lláh

3 'Izzat   *10 September*

As to the cycle of the Blessed Beauty – the times of the Greatest Name – this is not limited to a thousand or two thousand years . . .

When it is said that the period of a thousand years beginneth with the Manifestation of the Blessed Beauty and every day thereof is a thousand years, the intent is a reference to the cycle of the Blessed Beauty, which in this context will extend over many ages into the unborn reaches of time.

'Abdu'l-Bahá

4 'Izzat   *11 September*

O SERVANT of God! We have noted what thou didst write to Jináb-i-Ibn-Abhar, and thy question regarding the verse: 'Whoso layeth claim to a Revelation direct from God, ere the expiration of a full thousand years, such a man is assuredly a lying impostor.'

The meaning of this is that any individual who, before the expiry of a full thousand years – years known and clearly established by common usage and requiring no interpretation – should lay claim to a Revelation direct from God, even though he should reveal certain signs, that man is assuredly false and an impostor.

'Abdu'l-Bahá

5 'Izzat   12 September

CENTURIES, nay, countless ages, must pass away ere the Day-Star of Truth shineth again in its mid-summer splendour, or appeareth once more in the radiance of its vernal glory.

'Abdu'l-Bahá

6 'Izzat   13 September

. . . it is clearly set forth in the Holy Writings that centuries, nay thousands of years, must pass on to completion, before a Manifestation like unto this Manifestation shall appear again.

'Abdu'l-Bahá

7 'Izzat   14 September

MY purpose is this, that ere the expiration of a thousand years, no one has the right to utter a single word, even to claim the station of Guardianship. The Most Holy Book is the Book to which all the peoples shall refer, and in it the Laws of God have been revealed. Laws not mentioned in the Book should be referred to the decision of the Universal House of Justice. There will be no grounds for differences . . . Beware, beware lest anyone create a rift or stir up sedition. Should there be differences of opinion, the Supreme House of Justice would immediately resolve the problems. Whatever will be its decision, by majority vote, shall be the real truth, inasmuch as that House is under the protection, unerring guidance, and care of the one true Lord. He shall guard it from error and will protect it under the wing of His sanctity and infallibility. He who opposes it is cast out and will eventually be of the defeated.

'Abdu'l-Bahá

8 'Izzat   15 September

THE substance is, that prior to the completion of a thousand years, no individual may presume to breathe a word. All must consider themselves to be of the order of subjects, submissive and obedient to the commandments of God and the laws of the House of Justice. Should any deviate by so much as a needle's point from the decrees of the Universal House of Justice, or falter in his compliance therewith, then is he of the outcast and rejected.

'Abdu'l-Bahá

9 'Izzat   16 September

IT is possible, however, that after the completion of a full thousand years, certain Holy Beings will be empowered to deliver a Revelation: this, however, will not be through a Universal Manifestation.

'Abdu'l-Bahá

10 'Izzat   17 September

CONCERNING the Manifestations that will come down in the future 'in the shadows of the clouds', know verily that in so far as their relation to the source of their inspiration is concerned they are under the shadow of the Ancient Beauty. In their relation, however, to the age in which they appear, each and every one of them 'doeth whatsoever He willeth'.

'Abdu'l-Bahá

11 'Izzat   18 September

GOD hath sent down His Messengers to succeed to Moses and Jesus, and He will continue to do so till 'the end that hath no end'; so that His grace may, from the heaven of Divine bounty, be continually vouchsafed to mankind.

Bahá'u'lláh

12 'Izzat   19 September

I AM not apprehensive for My own self; My fears are for Him Who will be sent down unto you after Me – Him Who will be invested with great sovereignty and mighty dominion.

Bahá'u'lláh

13 'Izzat   20 September

BY those words which I have revealed, Myself is not intended, but rather He Who will come after Me. To it is witness God, the All-Knowing. Deal not with Him as ye have dealt with Me.

Bahá'u'lláh

14 'Izzat   21 September

MIGHT *not the following passage of the Hidden Words be . . . construed as*

115

an allegorical allusion to the progressiveness of Divine Revelation and an admission by its Author that the Message with which He has been entrusted is not the final and ultimate expression of the will and guidance of the Almighty?

Shoghi Effendi

O SON OF JUSTICE!

In the night-season the beauty of the immortal Being hath repaired from the emerald height of fidelity unto the Sadratu'l-Muntahá, and wept with such a weeping that the concourse on high and the dwellers of the realms above wailed at His lamenting. Whereupon there was asked, Why the wailing and weeping? He made reply: As bidden I waited expectant upon the hill of faithfulness, yet inhaled not from them that dwell on earth the fragrance of fidelity. Then summoned to return I beheld, and lo! certain doves of holiness were sore tried within the claws of the dogs of earth. Thereupon the Maid of heaven hastened forth unveiled and resplendent from Her mystic mansion, and asked of their names, and all were told but one. And when urged, the first letter thereof was uttered, whereupon the dwellers of the celestial chambers rushed forth out of their habitation of glory. And whilst the second letter was pronounced they fell down, one and all, upon the dust. At that moment a voice was heard from the inmost shrine: 'Thus far and no farther.' Verily We bear witness to that which they have done and now are doing.

Bahá'u'lláh

15 'Izzat   22 September

WHEN the channel of the human soul is cleansed of all worldly and impeding attachments, it will unfailingly perceive the breath of the Beloved across immeasurable

116

distances, and will, led by its perfume, attain and enter the City of Certitude.

Therein he will discern the .wonders of His ancient Wisdom, and will perceive all the hidden teachings from the rustling leaves of the Tree that flourisheth in that City. With both his inner and outer ear, he will hear from its dust the hymns of glory and praise ascending unto the Lord of Lords, and with his inner eye will he discover the mysteries of 'return' and 'revival' . . .

They that valiantly labour in quest of God, will, when once they have renounced all else but Him, be so attached and wedded unto that City, that a moment's separation from it would to them be unthinkable. They will hearken unto infallible proofs from the Hyacinth of that assembly, and will receive the surest testimonies from the beauty of its Rose, and the melody of its Nightingale. Once in about a thousand years shall this City be renewed and readorned . . .

That City is none other than the Word of God revealed in every age and dispensation.

Bahá'u'lláh

16 'Izzat   23 September

VERILY God will raise up Him Whom God shall make manifest, and after Him Whomsoever He willeth, even as He hath raised up prophets before the Point of the Bayán. He in truth hath power over all things.

The Báb

17 'Izzat   24 September

WE, verily, believe in Him Who, in the person of the Báb, hath been sent down by the Will of the one true God, the King of Kings, the All-Praised. We, moreover, swear fealty to the One Who, in the time of Mustag͟hát͟h, is destined to be made manifest, as well as to those Who shall come after Him till the end that hath no end. We recognize in the manifestation of each one of them, whether outwardly or inwardly, the manifestation of none but God Himself, if ye be of those that comprehend. Every one of them is a mirror of God, reflecting naught else but His Self, His Beauty, His Might and Glory, if ye will understand. All else besides them are to be regarded as mirrors capable of reflecting the glory of these Manifestations Who are themselves the Primary Mirrors of the Divine Being, if ye be not devoid of understanding. No one hath ever escaped them, neither are they to be hindered from achieving their purpose. These Mirrors will everlastingly succeed each other, and will continue to reflect the light of the Ancient of Days. They that reflect their glory will, in like manner, continue to exist for evermore, for the Grace of God can never cease from flowing. This is a truth that none can disprove.

Bahá'u'lláh

18 'Izzat   25 September

CAN one of sane mind ever seriously imagine that, in view of certain words the meaning of which he cannot comprehend, the portal of God's infinite guidance can ever be closed in the face of men? Can he ever conceive for these Divine Luminaries, these resplendent Lights either a beginning or an end? What outpouring flood can compare with the stream of His all-embracing grace, and what blessing can excel the evidences of so great and pervasive a mercy? There can be no doubt whatever that if for one moment the tide of His mercy and grace were to be withheld from the world, it would completely perish. For this reason, from the beginning that hath no beginning the portals of Divine mercy have been flung open to the face of all created things, and the clouds of Truth will continue to the end that hath no end to rain on the soil of human capacity, reality and personality their favours and bounties. Such hath been God's method continued from everlasting to everlasting.

Bahá'u'lláh

19 'Izzat   26 September

KNOW verily that the veil hiding Our countenance hath not been completely lifted. We have revealed Our Self to a degree corresponding to the capacity of the people of Our age. Should the Ancient Beauty be unveiled in the fullness of His glory mortal eyes would be blinded by the dazzling intensity of His revelation.

Bahá'u'lláh

The month of Ma<u>sh</u>íyyat begins at sunset.

11

Mashíyyat
(Will)

The Nature of the Covenant

Feast of Ma<u>sh</u>íyyat

1 Ma<u>sh</u>íyyat   27 September

HE is indeed a true believer in the unity of God who, in this
Day, will regard Him as One immeasurably exalted above
all the comparisons and likenesses with which men have
compared Him. He hath erred grievously who hath mistaken
these comparisons and likenesses for God Himself.

Bahá'u'lláh

2 Ma<u>sh</u>íyyat   28 September

OUR purpose in revealing these words is to show that the one
true God hath, in His all-highest and transcendent station,
ever been, and will everlastingly continue to be, exalted
above the praise and conception of all else but Him. His
creation hath ever existed, and the Manifestations of His
Divine glory and the Day Springs of eternal holiness have
been sent down from time immemorial, and been commissioned to summon mankind to the one true God.

Bahá'u'lláh

3 Ma<u>sh</u>íyyat 29 September

KNOW assuredly that just as thou firmly believest that the Word of God, exalted be His glory, endureth for ever, thou must, likewise, believe with undoubting faith that its meaning can never be exhausted. They who are its appointed interpreters, they whose hearts are the repositories of its secrets, are, however, the only ones who can comprehend its manifold wisdom.

Bahá'u'lláh

4 Ma<u>sh</u>íyyat 30 September

AND since there can be no tie of direct intercourse to bind the one true God with His creation, and no resemblance whatever can exist between the transient and the Eternal, the contingent and the Absolute, He hath ordained that in every age and dispensation a pure and stainless Soul be made manifest in the kingdoms of earth and heaven. Unto this subtle, this mysterious and ethereal Being He hath assigned a twofold nature; the physical, pertaining to the world of matter, and the spiritual, which is born of the substance of God Himself.

Bahá'u'lláh

5 Ma<u>sh</u>íyyat 1 October

SAY: O people, praise ye God, for its Manifestation, for verily it is the most great favour upon you and the most perfect blessing upon you; and through Him every mouldering bone is quickened. Whosoever turns to Him hath surely turned unto God, and whosoever turneth away from Him hath turned away from My beauty, denied My proof, and is of those who transgress. Verily, He is the remembrance of God amongst you and His trust within you, and His manifestation unto you and His appearance among the servants who are nigh. Thus have I been commanded to convey to you the message of God, your Creator; and I have delivered to you that of which I was commanded. Whereupon, thereunto testifieth God, then His angels, then His messengers, and then His holy servants.

Bahá'u'lláh

6 Mashíyyat   2 October

GOD leaves not His children comfortless, but, when the darkness of winter overshadows them, then again He sends His Messengers, the Prophets, with a renewal of the blessed spring. The Sun of Truth appears again on the horizon of the world shining into the eyes of those who sleep, awaking them to behold the glory of a new dawn. Then again will the tree of humanity blossom and bring forth the fruit of righteousness for the healing of the nations.

'Abdu'l-Bahá

7 Mashíyyat   3 October

GOD's eternal Mercy is immeasurable. He has always chosen certain souls upon whom He has shed the Divine Bounty of His heart, whose minds He has illumined with celestial light, to whom He has revealed the sacred mysteries, and kept clear before their sight the Mirror of Truth. These are the disciples of God, and His goodness has no bounds.

'Abdu'l-Bahá

8 Mashíyyat   4 October

. . . the Spiritual Teacher is the first to follow His own teaching; He brings down into the world of action His spiritual conceptions and ideals. His Divine thoughts are made manifest to the world. His thought is Himself, from which He is inseparable.

'Abdu'l-Bahá

9 Mashíyyat   5 October

VERILY, God effecteth that which He pleaseth . . . naught can obstruct His favour nor oppose His Cause! He doeth with all His Will that which pleaseth Him and He is powerful over all things!

'Abdu'l-Bahá

10 Mashíyyat   6 October

SAY, O peoples of the world! Do ye dispute with Me about God by virtue of the names which ye and your fathers have adopted for Him at the promptings of the Evil One? God hath indeed sent down this Book unto Me with truth that ye may be enabled to recognize the true names of God, inasmuch as ye have strayed in error far from the Truth. Verily We have taken a covenant from every created thing upon its coming into being concerning the Remembrance of God, and there shall be none to avert the binding command of God for the purification of mankind, as ordained in the Book which is written by the hand of the Báb.

The Báb

11 Mashíyyat   7 October

THROUGH the power of the divine springtime, the downpour
of the celestial clouds and the heat of the Sun of Reality, the
tree of life is just beginning to grow. Before long, it will
produce buds, bring forth leaves and fruits, and cast its
shade over the East and the West. This Tree of Life is the
Book of the Covenant.

'Abdu'l-Bahá

12 Mashíyyat   8 October

THE Lord, the All-Glorified, hath, beneath the shade of the
Tree of Anísá (Tree of Life), made a new Covenant and
established a great Testament . . . Hath such a Covenant
been established in any previous Dispensation, age, period,
or century, hath such a Testament, set down by the Pen of
the Most High, ever been witnessed? No, by God!

'Abdu'l-Bahá

13 Mashíyyat   9 October

THE lamp of the Covenant is the light of the world, and the
words traced by the Pen of the Most High a limitless ocean.

Bahá'u'lláh

14 Mashíyyat   10 October

KNOW thou that the 'Sure Handle' mentioned from the
foundation of the world in the Books, the Tablets, and the

Scriptures of old, is naught else but the Covenant and the Testament.

Bahá'u'lláh

15 Ma<u>sh</u>íyyat   11 October

THE Covenant of God . . . is a lifeboat and ark of salvation. All true followers of the Blessed Perfection are sheltered and protected in this ark. Whoever leaves it, trusting in his own will and strength, will drown and be destroyed.

'Abdu'l-Bahá

16 Ma<u>sh</u>íyyat   12 October

THE Covenant of God is like unto a vast and fathomless ocean. A billow shall rise and surge therefrom and shall cast ashore all accumulated foam.

'Abdu'l-Bahá

17 Ma<u>sh</u>íyyat   13 October

THE Covenant is like the sea and the believers as the fishes in the sea. If a fish leaves the water it cannot live. There is nothing to equal, nothing so effective as the Covenant of God to bring about and continue unity . . .

'Abdu'l-Bahá

18 Ma<u>sh</u>íyyat   14 October

. . . the ocean of the Covenant is tumultuous and wide. It

casteth ashore the foam of violation and thus rest ye assured.

'Abdu'l-Bahá

19 Ma<u>sh</u>íyyat   15 October

EVERYTHING is subject to corruption; but the Covenant of thy Lord shall continue to pervade all regions.

'Abdu'l-Bahá

The month of 'Ilm begins at sunset.

12

'Ilm
(Knowledge)

The Purpose of the Covenant

Feast of 'Ilm

1 'Ilm   16 October

O YE children of men! The fundamental purpose animating
the Faith of God and His Religion is to safeguard the
interests and promote the unity of the human race, and to
foster the spirit of love and fellowship amongst men . . .
This is the straight Path, the fixed and immovable foundation. Whatsoever is raised on this foundation, the changes
and chances of the world can never impair its strength, nor
will the revolution of countless centuries undermine its
structure.

Bahá'u'lláh

2 'Ilm   17 October

O YE that dwell on earth! The distinguishing feature that
marketh the preeminent character of this Supreme Revelation consisteth in that We have, on the one hand, blotted
out from the pages of God's holy Book whatsoever hath
been the cause of strife, of malice and mischief amongst the
children of men, and have, on the other, laid down the

essential prerequisites of concord, of understanding, of complete and enduring unity. Well is it with them that keep My statutes.

Bahá'u'lláh

3 'Ilm   18 October

Is it not the object of every Revelation to effect a transformation in the whole character of mankind, a transformation that shall manifest itself both outwardly and inwardly, that shall affect both its inner life and external conditions? For if the character of mankind be not changed, the futility of God's Universal Manifestation would be apparent.

Bahá'u'lláh

4 'Ilm   19 October

MY object is none other than the betterment of the world and the tranquillity of its peoples.

Bahá'u'lláh

The commemoration of the Birth of the Báb begins at sunset.

The Birth of the Báb

5 'Ilm   20 October

O THOU Who art the Lord of Lords! I testify that Thou art the Lord of all creation, and the Educator of all beings, visible and invisible. I bear witness that Thy power hath encompassed the entire universe, and that the hosts of the earth can never dismay Thee, nor can the dominion of all peoples and nations deter Thee from executing Thy purpose. I confess that Thou hast no desire except the regeneration of the whole world, and the establishment of the unity of its peoples, and the salvation of all them that dwell therein.

Bahá'u'lláh

6 'Ilm   21 October

IF any man were to meditate on that which the Scriptures, sent down from the heaven of God's holy Will, have revealed, he would readily recognize that their purpose is that all men shall be regarded as one soul, so that the seal bearing the words 'The Kingdom shall be God's' may be stamped on every heart, and the light of Divine bounty, of grace, and mercy may envelop all mankind.

Bahá'u'lláh

7 'Ilm   22 October

THE aim of the appearance of the Blessed Perfection – may my life be a sacrifice for His beloved ones! – was the unity and agreement of all the people of the world. Therefore, my utmost desire, firstly, is the accord and union and love of the believers and after that of all the people of the world.

'Abdu'l-Bahá

8 'Ilm   23 October

RELIGION should unite all hearts and cause wars and disputes to vanish from the face of the earth, give birth to spirituality, and bring life and light to each heart.

'Abdu'l-Bahá

9 *'Ilm*   *24 October*

THE purpose of the Blessed Beauty in entering into this Covenant and Testament was to gather all existent beings around one point so that the thoughtless souls, who in every cycle and generation have been the cause of dissension, may not undermine the Cause. He hath, therefore, commanded that whatever emanateth from the Centre of the Covenant is right and is under His protection and favour, while all else is error.

Praise be to God, thou art firm in the Covenant and the Testament.

'Abdu'l-Bahá

10 *'Ilm*   *25 October*

As to the most great characteristic of the revelation of Bahá'u'lláh, a specific teaching not given by any of the Prophets of the past: It is the ordination and appointment of the Centre of the Covenant. By this appointment and provision He has safeguarded and protected the religion of God against differences and schisms, making it impossible for anyone to create a new sect or faction of belief.

'Abdu'l-Bahá

11 *'Ilm*   *26 October*

To ensure unity and agreement He has entered into a

Covenant with all the people of the world, including the interpreter and explainer of His teachings, so that no one may interpret or explain the religion of God according to his own view or opinion and thus create a sect founded upon his individual understanding of the divine Words. The Book of the Covenant or Testament of Bahá'u'lláh is the means of preventing such a possibility, for whosoever shall speak from the authority of himself alone shall be degraded. Be ye informed and cognizant of this.

'Abdu'l-Bahá

12 *'Ilm*   27 October

INASMUCH as great differences and divergences of denominational belief had arisen throughout the past, every man with a new idea attributing it to God, Bahá'u'lláh desired that there should not be any ground or reason for disagreement among the Bahá'ís. Therefore, with His own pen He wrote the Book of His Covenant, addressing His relations and all people of the world, saying: 'Verily, I have appointed One who is the Centre of My Covenant. All must obey Him; all must turn to Him; He is the Expounder of My Book, and He is informed of My purpose.'

'Abdu'l-Bahá

13 *'Ilm*   28 October

UPON one occasion He asked His disciples, 'Whom say ye that I am?' Simon Peter answered and said, 'Thou art the Christ, the Son of the living God.' Christ, wishing to make firm the faith of Peter, said, 'Thou art Peter, and upon this rock I will build my church,' meaning that the faith of Peter was the true faith. It was a sanction of Peter's faith. He did not say that all should turn to Peter. He did not say, 'He is the branch extended from my ancient root.' He did not say, 'O God! Bless all who serve Peter. O God! Degrade those who are not obedient to him. Shun him who is a violator of the Covenant. O God! Thou knowest that I love all who are steadfast in the Covenant.' This has been revealed, however, in all the Books, Writings and Epistles of Bahá'u'lláh regarding the appointed Centre of the Covenant in this dispensation. Therefore, the Bahá'í dispensation is distinguished from all others in this fact, the purpose of Bahá'u'lláh being that no one could arise to cause differences and disunion.

'Abdu'l-Bahá

14 'Ilm   29 October

THEREFORE, thank God that Bahá'u'lláh has made the pathway straight. He has clearly explained all things and opened every door for advancing souls. There is no reason for hesitation by anyone. The purpose of the Covenant was simply to ward off disunion and differences so that no one might say, 'My opinion is the true and valid one.'

'Abdu'l-Bahá

15 'Ilm   30 October

TODAY no power can conserve the oneness of the Bahá'í world save the Covenant of God; otherwise differences like unto a most great tempest will encompass the Bahá'í world.

'Abdu'l-Bahá

16 'Ilm   31 October

So intensely hath the glory of Divine Unity penetrated souls and hearts that all are now bound one to another with heavenly ties, and all are even as a single heart, a single soul. Wherefore reflections of the spirit and impressions of the Divine are now mirrored clear and sharp in the deep heart's core. I beg of God to strengthen these spiritual bonds as day followeth day, and make this mystic oneness to shine ever more brightly, until at last all shall be as troops marshalled together beneath the banner of the Covenant within the sheltering shade of the Word of God; that they may strive with all their might until universal fellowship, close and warm, and unalloyed love, and spiritual relationships, will connect all the hearts in the world. Then will all humankind, because of this fresh and dazzling bounty, be gathered in a single homeland. Then will conflict and dissension vanish from the face of the earth, then will mankind be cradled in love for the beauty of the All-Glorious.

'Abdu'l-Bahá

17 'Ilm   1 November

HAD the Covenant not come to pass, had it not been revealed from the Supreme Pen and had not the Book of the Covenant like unto the ray of the Sun of Reality, illuminated the world, the forces of the Cause of God would have been utterly scattered and certain souls who were the prisoners of their own passions and lusts would have taken into their hands an axe, cutting the root of this Blessed Tree. Every person would have pushed forward his own desire and every individual aired his own opinion!

'Abdu'l-Bahá

18 'Ilm   2 November

Do not disrupt Bahá'í unity, and know that this unity cannot be maintained save through faith in the Covenant of God.

'Abdu'l-Bahá

19 'Ilm   3 November

SAY: Oh servants! Do not make the cause of order a cause for disorder, nor the means of unity a means for disunity. It is hoped that the people of Bahá will observe the sacred verse: 'Say, all are created by God.' This lofty utterance is like unto water for quenching the fire of hate and hostility which is hidden and stored in men's hearts and minds. This single utterance will cause the various sects and creeds to attain the light of true unity. Verily, He speaketh truth and guideth to the right path; and He is the Mighty, the Glorious, the Omnipotent.

Bahá'u'lláh

The month of Qudrat begins at sunset.

13

Qudrat
(Power)

The Power of the Covenant

Feast of Qudrat

1 Qudrat   4 November

ALL-PRAISE to Him Who, by the Shield of His Covenant, hath guarded the Temple of His Cause from the darts of doubtfulness, Who by the Hosts of His Testament hath preserved the Sanctuary of His Most Beneficent Law and protected His Straight and Luminous Path, staying thereby the onslaught of the company of Covenant-breakers, that have threatened to subvert His Divine Edifice; Who hath watched over His Mighty Stronghold and All-glorious Faith, through the aid of men whom the slander of the slanderer affect not, whom no earthly calling, glory, and power can turn aside from the Covenant of God and His Testament, established firmly by His clear and manifest words, writ and revealed by His All-Glorious Pen and recorded in the Preserved Tablet.

'Abdu'l-Bahá

2 Qudrat   5 November

THERE is a power in this Cause – a mysterious power – far,

143

far, far away from the ken of men and angels; that invisible power is the cause of all these outward activities. It moves the hearts. It rends the mountains. It administers the complicated affairs of the Cause. It inspires the friends. It dashes into a thousand pieces all the forces of opposition. It creates new spiritual worlds. This is the mystery of the Kingdom of Abhá!

'Abdu'l-Bahá

3 Qudrat   6 November

IT is indubitably clear that the pivot of the oneness of mankind is nothing else but the power of the Covenant.

'Abdu'l-Bahá

4 Qudrat   7 November

IT is evident that the axis of the oneness of the world of humanity is the power of the Covenant and nothing else.

'Abdu'l-Bahá

5 Qudrat   8 November

THE power of the Covenant is as the heat of the sun which quickeneth and promoteth the development of all created things on earth. The light of the Covenant, in like manner, is the educator of the minds, the spirits, the hearts and souls of men.

'Abdu'l-Bahá

6 Qudrat   9 November

BUT this power of the Covenant shall heat every freezing soul, shall bestow light upon everything that is dark and shall secure for the captive in the hand of nature the true freedom of the Kingdom.

'Abdu'l-Bahá

7 Qudrat   10 November

O THOU daughter of the Kingdom! Thy letter was received. It was like the melody of the divine nightingale, whose song delighteth the hearts. This is because its contents indicated faith, assurance and firmness in the Covenant and the Testament. Today the dynamic power of the world of existence is the power of the Covenant which like unto an artery pulsateth in the body of the contingent world and protecteth Bahá'í unity.

The Bahá'ís are commanded to establish the oneness of mankind; if they cannot unite around one point how will they be able to bring about the unity of mankind?

'Abdu'l-Bahá

8 Qudrat   11 November

TODAY, every wise, vigilant and foresighted person is awakened, and to him are unveiled the mysteries of the future which show that nothing save the power of the Covenant is able to stir and move the heart of humanity, just as the New and Old Testaments propounded throughout all regions the Cause of Christ and were the pulsating power in the body of the human world. A tree that hath a root shall

145

bear fruit, while the tree that hath none, no matter how high and hardy it may be, will eventually wither, perish and become but a log fit for the fire.

'Abdu'l-Bahá

The anniversary of the Birth of Bahá'u'lláh begins at sunset.

The Birth of Bahá'u'lláh

9 Qudrat   12 November

TODAY, the Lord of Hosts is the defender of the Covenant, the forces of the Kingdom protect it, heavenly souls tender their services, and heavenly angels promulgate and spread it broadcast. If it is considered with insight, it will be seen that all the forces of the universe, in the last analysis, serve the Covenant.

'Abdu'l-Bahá

10 Qudrat   13 November

THE first condition is firmness in the Covenant of God. For the power of the Covenant will protect the Cause of Bahá'u'lláh from the doubts of the people of error. It is the fortified fortress of the Cause of God and the firm pillar of the religion of God.

'Abdu'l-Bahá

11 Qudrat   14 November

O YE My Branches! A mighty force, a consummate power

lieth concealed in the world of being. Fix your gaze upon it and upon its unifying influence, and not upon the differences which appear from it.

Bahá'u'lláh

12 Qudrat   15 November

WERE it not for the protecting power of the Covenant to guard the impregnable fort of the Cause of God, there would arise among the Bahá'ís, in one day, a thousand different sects as was the case in former ages.

'Abdu'l-Bahá

13 Qudrat   16 November

KNOW this for a certainty that today, the penetrative power in the arteries of the world of humanity is the power of the Covenant. The body of the world will not be moved through any power except through the power of the Covenant. There is no other power like unto this. This Spirit of the Covenant is the real Centre of love and is reflecting its rays to all parts of the globe, which are resuscitating and regenerating man and illuminating the path to the Divine Kingdom.

'Abdu'l-Bahá

14 Qudrat   17 November

VERILY, God effecteth that which He pleaseth; naught can annul His Covenant; naught can obstruct His favour nor oppose His Cause! He doeth with all His Will that which pleaseth Him and He is powerful over all things!

'Abdu'l-Bahá

15 Qudrat   18 November

TODAY the pulsating power in the arteries of the body of the world is the spirit of the Covenant – the spirit which is the cause of life. Whosoever is vivified with this spirit, the freshness and beauty of life become manifest in him, he is baptized with the Holy Spirit, he is born again, is freed from oppression and tyranny, from heedlessness and harshness which deaden the spirit, and attains to everlasting life.

Praise thou God that thou art firm in the Covenant and the Testament and art turning thy face to the Luminary of the world, His Highness Bahá'u'lláh.

'Abdu'l-Bahá

16 Qudrat   19 November

HOW great, how very great is the Cause! How very fierce the onslaught of all the peoples and kindreds of the earth. Ere long shall the clamour of the multitude throughout Africa, throughout America, the cry of the European and of the Turk, the groaning of India and China, be heard from far and near. One and all, they shall arise with all their power to resist His Cause. Then shall the knights of the Lord, assisted by His grace from on high, strengthened by faith, aided by the power of understanding, and reinforced by the legions of the Covenant, arise and make manifest the truth of the verse: 'Behold the confusion that hath befallen the tribes of the defeated!'

'Abdu'l-Bahá

17 Qudrat   20 November

THE tests of every dispensation are in direct proportion to the greatness of the Cause, and as heretofore such a manifest Covenant, written by the Supreme Pen, hath not been entered upon, the tests are proportionately more severe. These trials cause the feeble souls to waver whilst those who are firm are not affected. These agitations of the violators are no more than the foam of the ocean, which is one of its inseparable features; but the ocean of the Covenant shall surge and shall cast ashore the bodies of the dead, for it cannot retain them. Thus it is seen that the ocean of the Covenant hath surged and surged until it hath thrown out the dead bodies – souls that are deprived of the Spirit of God and are lost in passion and self and are seeking leadership. This foam of the ocean shall not endure and shall soon disperse and vanish, while the ocean of the Covenant shall eternally surge and roar . . .

'Abdu'l-Bahá

18 Qudrat   21 November

SAY: Beware, O people of Bahá, lest the strong ones of the earth rob you of your strength, or they who rule the world fill you with fear. Put your trust in God, and commit your affairs to His keeping. He, verily, will, through the power of truth, render you victorious, and He, verily, is powerful to do what He willeth, and in His grasp are the reins of omnipotent might.

Bahá'u'lláh

19 Qudrat   22 November

O THOU who warmest thyself by the fire of the love of God,

spreading from the Tree of the Covenant! Let thy soul be at ease and thy heart in peace concerning the perfect success and progress which the pen is not able to express, for in a short time thou shalt see the flag of the Kingdom waving in those far and wide regions, and the lights of the Truth shining brilliantly in its dawn above those horizons, and thou shalt know that thou art the centre of the circle of the love of God, the axis around which souls revolve in their way and supplication to God. Therefore, thou must widen thy heart, dilate thy breast, have patience in plenty, calmness of soul and cut thyself from everything but God!

'Abdu'l-Bahá

The month of Qawl begins at sunset.

14

Qawl
(Speech)

The Call to Firmness in the Covenant

Feast of Qawl

1 Qawl   23 November

THE first and foremost duty prescribed unto men, next to the recognition of Him Who is the Eternal Truth, is the duty of steadfastness in His Cause. Cleave thou unto it, and be of them whose minds are firmly fixed and grounded in God. No act, however meritorious, did or can ever compare unto it. It is the king of all acts, and to this thy Lord, the All-Highest, the Most Powerful, will testify.

Bahá'u'lláh

2 Qawl   24 November

A TWOFOLD obligation resteth upon him who hath recognized the Day Spring of the Unity of God, and acknowledged the truth of Him Who is the Manifestation of His oneness. The first is steadfastness in His love, such steadfastness that neither the clamour of the enemy nor the claims of the idle pretender can deter him from cleaving unto Him Who is the Eternal Truth, a steadfastness that taketh no account of them whatever. The second is strict observance of the laws

153

He hath prescribed – laws which He hath always ordained, and will continue to ordain, unto men, and through which the truth may be distinguished and separated from falsehood.

Bahá'u'lláh

3 Qawl   25 November

IN the Name of God, the Peerless! O handmaid of God! Steadfastness in the Cause is mentioned in the Tablets and set forth by the Pen of the Ancient of Days. Render thanks to the Beloved of the world that thou hast set thy heart on Him and art uttering His praise.

Bahá'u'lláh

The celebration of the Day of the Covenant begins at sunset.

Day of the Covenant

4 Qawl   26 November

O YE beloved of God, know that steadfastness and firmness in this new and wonderful Covenant is indeed the spirit that quickeneth the hearts which are overflowing with the love of the Glorious Lord; verily, it is the power which penetrates into the hearts of the people of the world! Your Lord hath assuredly promised His servants who are firm and steadfast to render them victorious at all times, to exalt their word, propagate their power, diffuse their lights, strengthen their hearts, elevate their banners, assist their hosts, brighten their stars, increase the abundance of the showers of mercy

154

upon them, and enable the brave lions (teachers of the Cause) to conquer.

Hasten, hasten, O ye firm believers! Hasten, hasten, O ye steadfast! Abandon the heedless, set aside every ignorant, take hold of the strong rope, be firm in this Great Cause, draw light from this Evident Light, be patient and be steadfast in this wise Religion! Ye shall see the hosts of inspiration descending successively from the Supreme World, the procession of attraction falling incessantly from the heights of heaven, the abundance of the Kingdom of El-Abhá outpouring continually and the teachings of God penetrating with the utmost power, while the heedless are indeed in evident loss.

'Abdu'l-Bahá

5 Qawl   27 November

HOLD thou fast to the Covenant of thy Lord, and as the days go by, increase thy store of love for His beloved ones. Bend thou with tenderness over the servitors of the All-Merciful, that thou mayest hoist the sail of love upon the ark of peace that moveth across the seas of life. Let nothing grieve thee, and be thou angered at none. It behoveth thee to be content with the Will of God, and a true and loving and trusted friend to all the peoples of the earth, without any exceptions whatever. This is the quality of the sincere, the way of the saints, the emblem of those who believe in the unity of God, and the raiment of the people of Bahá.

'Abdu'l-Bahá

The commemoration of the anniversary of the Ascension of 'Abdu'l-Bahá begins at sunset.

Ascension of 'Abdu'l-Bahá

6 Qawl   *28 November*

AND now I give you a commandment which shall be for a
covenant between you and Me – that ye have faith; that your
faith be steadfast as a rock that no storms can move, that
nothing can disturb, and that it endure through all things
even to the end; even should ye hear that your Lord has
been crucified, be not shaken in your faith; for I am with you
always, whether living or dead, I am with you to the end. As
ye have faith so shall your powers and blessings be. This is
the balance – this is the balance – this is the balance.

'Abdu'l-Bahá

*The Ascension of 'Abdu'l-Bahá is commemorated at one o'clock in the
morning on this day.*

7 Qawl   *29 November*

THEREFORE, in the beginning one must make his steps firm in
the Covenant so that the confirmations of Bahá'u'lláh may
encircle from all sides, the cohorts of the Supreme Concourse may become the supporters and the helpers, and the
exhortations and advices of 'Abdu'l-Bahá, like unto the
pictures engraved on stone, may remain permanent and
ineffaceable in the tablets of the hearts.

'Abdu'l-Bahá

8 Qawl   *30 November*

THE necessity and the particularity of the assured and

believing ones is to be firm in the Cause of God and with-stand the hidden and evident tests. Thanks be to God that you are distinguished and made eminent by this blessing.

'Abdu'l-Bahá

9 Qawl   1 December

TODAY the most important principle of faith is firmness in the Covenant, because firmness in the Covenant wards off differences. Therefore, you must be firm as mountains.

'Abdu'l-Bahá

10 Qawl   2 December

BLESSED art thou, O Vafá, inasmuch as thou hast been faithful to the Covenant of God and His Testament at a time when all men have violated it and have repudiated the One in Whom they had believed, and this notwithstanding that He hath appeared invested with every testimony, and hath dawned from the horizon of Revelation clothed with undoubted sovereignty.

It behoveth thee, however, to exert thine utmost to attain the very essence of fidelity. This implieth to be well assured in thy heart and to testify with thy tongue to that whereunto God hath testified for His Own exalted Self, proclaiming: 'Verily, self-subsisting am I within the Realm of Glory.' Whoso is enabled in these days to solemnly affirm this truth, hath attained unto all good, and the heavenly Spirit shall descend upon him in the daytime and in the night season, shall graciously assist him to glorify the Name of his Lord and suffer him to unloose his tongue and uphold with his words the Cause of his Lord, the Merciful, the Compassionate. And none can ever achieve this except he who hath purged his heart from whatsoever is created between heaven and earth, and hath entirely detached himself from all but God, the sovereign Lord, the Almighty, the Gracious.

Bahá'u'lláh

11 Qawl   3 December

TAKE the cup of the Testament in thy hand; leap and dance with ecstasy in the triumphal procession of the Covenant! Lay your confidence in the everlasting bounty, turn to the presence of the generous God; ask assistance from the Kingdom of Abhá; seek confirmation from the Supreme World; turn thy vision to the horizon of eternal wealth; and pray for help from the Source of Mercy!

'Abdu'l-Bahá

12 Qawl   4 December

FIRMNESS in the Covenant means obedience so that no one may say, 'this is my opinion,' nay rather he must obey that which proceeds from the Pen and Tongue of the Covenant.

'Abdu'l-Bahá

13 Qawl   5 December

O MY servants! There shineth nothing else in Mine heart except the unfading light of the Morn of Divine guidance, and out of My mouth proceedeth naught but the essence of truth, which the Lord your God hath revealed. Follow not, therefore, your earthly desires, and violate not the Covenant of God, nor break your pledge to Him. With firm determination, with the whole affection of your heart, and with the full force of your words, turn ye unto Him, and walk not in the ways of the foolish. The world is but a show, vain and empty, a mere nothing, bearing the semblance of reality. Set not your affections upon it. Break not the bond that uniteth you with your Creator, and be not of those that have erred and strayed from His ways.

Bahá'u'lláh

14 Qawl   6 December

SAY! Fear God, O people, and follow not the doubts of such as shout aloud, who have broken the Covenant of God and His Testament, and denied His mercy that hath preceded all that are in the heavens and all that are on earth.

Bahá'u'lláh

15 Qawl   7 December

O YE servants! There is nothing in this heart save the effulgences of the splendour of the morn of Meeting, and it does not speak but the absolute truth from your Lord. Therefore, do not follow self; break not God's Covenant and violate not His Testament. Proceed with perfect steadfastness, and with heart, soul and tongue, turn unto Him, and be not of the thoughtless.

'Abdu'l-Bahá

16 Qawl   8 December

PRAISE be to God, ye are firm and steadfast; be ye thankful that like unto blessed trees ye are firmly planted in the soil of the Covenant. It is sure that every firm one will grow, will yield new fruits and will increase daily in freshness and grace. Reflect upon all the writings of Bahá'u'lláh, whether epistles or prayers, and ye shall surely come across a thousand passages wherein Bahá'u'lláh prays: 'O God! Bring to naught the violators of the Covenant and defeat the oppressors of the Testament.' 'He who denieth the Covenant and the Testament is rejected by God, and he who remaineth firm and steadfast therein is favoured at the Threshold of Oneness.' Such sayings and prayers abound, refer to them and ye shall know.

'Abdu'l-Bahá

17 Qawl   9 December

ENDEAVOUR, therefore, that ye may scatter and disperse the army of doubt and of error with the power of the holy utterances. This is my exhortation and this is my counsel. Do not quarrel with anybody, and shun every form of dispute. Utter the Word of God. If he accepteth it the desired purpose is attained, and if he turneth away leave him to himself and trust to God.

Such is the attribute of those who are firm in the Covenant.

'Abdu'l-Bahá

18 Qawl   10 December

O THOU who art enamoured of the Covenant! The Blessed

Beauty hath promised this servant that souls would be raised up who would be the very embodiments of guidance, and banners of the Concourse on high, torches of God's oneness, and stars of His pure truth, shining in the heavens where God reigneth alone. They would give sight to the blind, and would make the deaf to hear; they would raise the dead to life. They would confront all the peoples of the earth, pleading their Cause with proofs of the Lord of the seven spheres.

It is my hope that in His bounty He will soon raise up these souls, that His Cause may be exalted. The lodestone which will attract this grace is staunchness in the Covenant. Render thou thanks unto God that thou art firmest of the firm.

'Abdu'l-Bahá

19 Qawl   *11 December*

O THOU dear handmaid of God! Thy letter hath been received and its contents noted. Thou didst ask for a rule whereby to guide thy life.

Believe thou in God, and keep thine eyes fixed upon the exalted Kingdom; be thou enamoured of the Abhá Beauty; stand thou firm in the Covenant; yearn thou to ascend into the Heaven of the Universal Light. Be thou severed from this world, and reborn through the sweet scents of holiness that blow from the realm of the All-Highest. Be thou a summoner to love, and be thou kind to all the human race. Love thou the children of men and share in their sorrows. Be thou of those who foster peace. Offer thy friendship, be worthy of trust. Be thou a balm to every sore, be thou a medicine for every ill. Bind thou the souls together. Recite thou the verses of guidance. Be engaged in the worship of thy Lord, and rise up to lead the people aright. Loose thy tongue and teach, and let thy face be bright with the fire of God's love. Rest thou not for a moment, seek thou to draw no easeful breath. Thus mayest thou become a sign and symbol of God's love, and a banner of His grace.

'Abdu'l-Bahá

The month of Masá'il begins at sunset.

15

Masá'il
(Questions)

Bounties and Blessings of Firmness in the Covenant

Feast of Masá'il

1 Masá'il   12 December

BLESSED is he who hath remained faithful to My Covenant, and whom the things of the world have not kept back from attaining My Court of holiness.

Bahá'u'lláh

2 Masá'il   13 December

BESEECH ye the one true God to grant that ye may taste the savour of such deeds as are performed in His path, and partake of the sweetness of such humility and submissiveness as are shown for His sake . . . If ye follow in His way, His incalculable and imperishable blessings will be showered upon you.

Bahá'u'lláh

3 Masá'il   14 December

BLESSED is the servant or maid-servant who believes, and

woe to the polytheists who have violated the Covenant of God and His Testament, and deviated from My Right Path.

Bahá'u'lláh

4 *Masá'il*   15 *December*

O YE co-workers who are supported by armies from the realm of the All-Glorious! Blessed are ye, for ye have come together in the sheltering shade of the Word of God, and have found a refuge in the cave of His Covenant; ye have brought peace to your hearts by making your home in the Abhá Paradise, and are lulled by the gentle winds that blow from their source in His loving-kindness; ye have arisen to serve the Cause of God and to spread His religion far and wide, to promote His Word and to raise high the banners of holiness throughout all those regions.

'Abdu'l-Bahá

5 *Masá'il*   16 *December*

WE have admonished Our loved ones to fear God, a fear which is the fountainhead of all goodly deeds and virtues. It is the commander of the hosts of justice in the city of Bahá. Happy the man that hath entered the shadow of its luminous standard, and laid fast hold thereon. He, verily, is of the Companions of the Crimson Ark, which hath been mentioned in the Qayyúm-i-Asmá.

Bahá'u'lláh

6 *Masá'il*   17 *December*

O QURRATU'L-'AYN! Deliver the summons of the most

exalted Word unto the handmaids among Thy kindred, caution them against the Most Great Fire and announce unto them the joyful tidings that following this mighty Covenant there shall be everlasting reunion with God in the Paradise of His good-pleasure, nigh unto the Seat of Holiness. Verily God, the Lord of creation, is potent over all things.

The Báb

7 Masá'il   18 December

EVERY receptive soul who hath in this Day inhaled the fragrance of His garment and hath, with a pure heart, set his face towards the all-glorious Horizon is reckoned among the people of Bahá in the Crimson Book. Grasp ye, in My Name, the chalice of My loving-kindness, drink then your fill in My glorious and wondrous remembrance.

Bahá'u'lláh

8 Masá'il   19 December

SHARP must be thy sight . . . and adamant thy soul, and brass-like thy feet, if thou wishest to be unshaken by the assaults of the selfish desires that whisper in men's breasts . . . Whatever thou seest in this Day shall perish. Supremely lofty will be thy station, if thou remainest steadfast in the Cause of thy Lord.

Bahá'u'lláh

9 Masá'il   20 December

THE people of Bahá burn brightly amidst the gatherings even

as a candle and hold fast unto that which God hath purposed. This station standeth supreme above all stations. Well is it with him who hath cast away the things that the people of the world possess, yearning for that which pertaineth unto God, the Sovereign Lord of eternity.

Bahá'u'lláh

10 Masá'il   21 December

LOFTY is the station of man! Not long ago this exalted Word streamed forth from the treasury of Our Pen of Glory: Great and blessed is this Day – the Day in which all that lay latent in man hath been and will be made manifest. Lofty is the station of man, were he to hold fast to righteousness and truth and to remain firm and steadfast in the Cause. In the eyes of the All-Merciful a true man appeareth even as a firmament; its sun and moon are his sight and hearing, and his shining and resplendent character its stars. His is the loftiest station, and his influence educateth the world of being.

Bahá'u'lláh

11 Masá'il   22 December

THOSE who have been faithful to God's Covenant are of the highest ones in the sight of the exalted Lord. Those who have become negligent are of the people of fire in the sight of Thy Lord, the Beloved, the Independent.

Bahá'u'lláh

12 Masá'il   23 December

IF any man were to arise to defend, in his writings, the

Cause of God against its assailants, such a man, however inconsiderable his share, shall be so honoured in the world to come that the Concourse on high would envy his glory. No pen can depict the loftiness of his station, neither can any tongue describe its splendour. For whosoever standeth firm and steadfast in this holy, this glorious, and exalted Revelation, such power shall be given him as to enable him to face and withstand all that is in heaven and on earth. Of this God is Himself a witness.

Bahá'u'lláh

13 Masá'il   24 December

UNDER all conditions those who have remained firm in the Covenant have conquered, while the violators have met defeat, disappointment and dejection.

'Abdu'l-Bahá

14 Masá'il   25 December

WALK, therefore, with a sure step and engage with the utmost assurance and confidence in the promulgation of the divine fragrances, the glorification of the Word of God and firmness in the Covenant. Rest ye assured that if a soul ariseth in the utmost perseverance and raiseth the Call of the Kingdom and resolutely promulgateth the Covenant, be he an insignificant ant he shall be enabled to drive away the formidable elephant from the arena, and if he be a feeble moth he shall cut to pieces the plumage of the rapacious vulture.

'Abdu'l-Bahá

15 *Masá'il*   *26 December*

WERE men to strictly observe that which the Pen of the Most High hath revealed in the Crimson Book, they could then well afford to dispense with the regulations which prevail in the world. Certain exhortations have repeatedly streamed forth from the Pen of the Most High that perchance the manifestations of power and the dawning-places of might may, sometime, be enabled to enforce them. Indeed were sincere seekers to be found, every emanation of God's pervasive and irresistible Will would, for the sake of His love, be revealed. But where are to be found earnest seekers and inquiring minds? Whither are gone the equitable and the fair-minded?

Bahá'u'lláh

16 *Masá'il*   *27 December*

O YE League of the Covenant! Verily the Abhá Beauty made a promise to the beloved who are steadfast in the Covenant, that He would reinforce their strivings with the strongest of supports, and succour them with His triumphant might. Ere long shall ye see that your illumined assemblage hath left conspicuous signs and tokens in the hearts and souls of men. Hold ye fast to the hem of God's garment, and direct all your efforts toward furthering His Covenant, and burning ever more brightly with the fire of His love, that your hearts may leap for joy in the breathings of servitude which well out from the breast of 'Abdu'l-Bahá. Rally your hearts, make firm your steps, trust in the everlasting bounties that will be shed upon you, one following another from the Kingdom of Abhá. Whensoever ye gather in that radiant assemblage, know ye that the splendours of Bahá are shining over you.

'Abdu'l-Bahá

17 Masá'il   28 December

O YE who are firm in the Covenant! 'Abdu'l-Bahá is constantly engaged in ideal communication with any Spiritual Assembly which is instituted through the divine bounty, and the members of which, in the utmost devotion, turn to the divine Kingdom and are firm in the Covenant. To them he is whole-heartedly attached and with them he is linked by everlasting ties. Thus correspondence with that gathering is sincere, constant and uninterrupted.

At every instant, I beg for you assistance, bounty, and a fresh favour and blessing, so that the confirmations of Bahá'u'lláh may, like unto the sea, be constantly surging, the lights of the Sun of Truth may shine upon you all and that ye may be confirmed in service, may become the manifestations of bounty and that each one of you may, at dawn, turn unto the Holy Land and may experience spiritual emotions with all intensity.

'Abdu'l-Bahá

18 Masá'il   29 December

IF in this day a soul shall act according to the precepts and the counsels of God, he will serve as a divine physician to mankind, and like the trump of Isráfíl, he will call the dead of this contingent world to life; for the confirmations of the Abhá Realm are never interrupted, and such a virtuous soul hath, to befriend him, the unfailing help of the Company on high. Thus shall a sorry gnat become an eagle in the fullness of his strength, and a feeble sparrow change to a royal falcon in the heights of ancient glory.

'Abdu'l-Bahá

19 Masá'il   30 December

O SINCERE servant of the True One! I hear thou art grieved and distressed at the happenings of the world and the vicissitudes of fortune. Wherefore this fear and sorrow? The true lovers of the Abhá Beauty, and they that have quaffed the Cup of the Covenant fear no calamity, nor feel depressed in the hour of trial. They regard the fire of adversity as their garden of delight, and the depth of the sea the expanse of heaven.

Thou who art neath the shelter of God, and under the shadow of the Tree of His Covenant, why sorrow and repine? Rest thou assured and feel confident. Observe the written commandments of thy Lord with joy and peace, with earnestness and sincerity; and be thou the well-wisher of thy country and thy government. His grace shall assist thee at all times, His blessings shall be bestowed upon thee, and thy heart's desire shall be realized.

'Abdu'l-Bahá

The month of Sharaf begins at sunset.

16

Sharaf
(Honour)

Becoming Firm in the Covenant

Feast of Sharaf

1 Sharaf   *31 December*

WHATSOEVER the Creator commandeth His creatures to observe, the same must they diligently, and with the utmost joy and eagerness, arise and fulfil. They should in no wise allow their fancy to obscure their judgement, neither should they regard their own imaginings as the voice of the Eternal.

Bahá'u'lláh

2 Sharaf   *1 January*

O MY servants! My holy, My divinely ordained Revelation may be likened unto an ocean in whose depths are concealed innumerable pearls of great price, of surpassing lustre. It is the duty of every seeker to bestir himself and strive to attain the shores of this ocean, so that he may, in proportion to the eagerness of his search and the efforts he hath exerted, partake of such benefits as have been pre-ordained in God's irrevocable and hidden Tablets.

Bahá'u'lláh

3 <u>Sh</u>araf   2 January

RECITE ye the verses of God every morning and evening. Whoso reciteth them not hath truly failed to fulfil his pledge to the Covenant of God and His Testament and whoso in this day turneth away therefrom hath indeed turned away from God since time immemorial. Fear ye God, O concourse of My servants.

Bahá'u'lláh

4 <u>Sh</u>araf   3 January

THEY who are the beloved of God, in whatever place they gather and whomsoever they may meet, must evince, in their attitude towards God, and in the manner of their celebration of His praise and glory, such humility and submissiveness that every atom of the dust beneath their feet may attest the depth of their devotion.

Bahá'u'lláh

5 <u>Sh</u>araf   4 January

O OPPRESSORS ON EARTH!
Withdraw your hands from tyranny, for I have pledged Myself not to forgive any man's injustice. This is My covenant which I have irrevocably decreed in the preserved tablet and sealed it with My seal of glory.

Bahá'u'lláh

6 <u>Sh</u>araf   5 January

O ARMY of God! Through the protection and help vouch-

176

safed by the Blessed Beauty – may my life be a sacrifice to His loved ones – ye must conduct yourselves in such a manner that ye may stand out distinguished and brilliant as the sun among other souls. Should any one of you enter a city, he should become a centre of attraction by reason of his sincerity, his faithfulness and love, his honesty and fidelity, his truthfulness and loving-kindness towards all the peoples of the world, so that the people of that city may cry out and say: 'This man is unquestionably a Bahá'í, for his manners, his behaviour, his conduct, his morals, his nature, and disposition reflect the attributes of the Bahá'ís.' Not until ye attain this station can ye be said to have been faithful to the Covenant and Testament of God. For He hath, through irrefutable Texts, entered into a binding Covenant with us all, requiring us to act in accordance with His sacred instructions and counsels.

'Abdu'l-Bahá

7 Sharaf   6 January

LET God's beloved, each and every one, be the essence of purity, the very life of holiness, so that in every country they may become famed for their sanctity, independence of spirit, and meekness. Let them be cheered by draughts from the eternal cup of love for God, and make merry as they drink from the wine-vaults of Heaven. Let them behold the Blessed Beauty, and feel the flame and rapture of that meeting, and be struck dumb with awe and wonder. This is the station of the sincere; this is the way of the loyal; this is the brightness that shineth on the faces of those nigh unto God.

'Abdu'l-Bahá

8 <u>Sharaf</u>   7 January

. . . they should exemplify in every aspect of their lives those attributes and virtues that are born of God and should arise to distinguish themselves by their goodly behaviour. They should justify their claim to be Bahá'ís by deeds and not by name. He is a true Bahá'í who strives by day and by night to progress and advance along the path of human endeavour, whose most cherished desire is so to live and act as to enrich and illuminate the world, whose source of inspiration is the essence of Divine virtue, whose aim in life is so to conduct himself as to be the cause of infinite progress. Only when he attains unto such perfect gifts can it be said of him that he is a true Bahá'í. For in this holy Dispensation, the crowning glory of bygone ages and cycles, true Faith is no mere acknowledgement of the Unity of God, but rather the living of a life that will manifest all the perfections and virtues implied in such belief.

'Abdu'l-Bahá

9 <u>Sharaf</u>   8 January

O YE friends of God! Show ye an endeavour that all the nations and communities of the world, even the enemies, put their trust, assurance and hope in you; that if a person falls into errors for a hundred thousand times he may yet turn his face to you, hopeful that you will forgive his sins; for he must not become hopeless, neither grieved nor despondent. This is the conduct and the manner of the people of Bahá. This is the foundation of the most high pathway! Ye should conform your conduct and manners with the advices of 'Abdu'l-Bahá.

'Abdu'l-Bahá

10 <u>Sh</u>araf   9 January

THEN know thou that, verily, the people of Bahá must needs be distinguished from others in all respects, until they become the lamps of the True One among the creatures and the stars of guidance shining from the Supreme Concourse.

'Abdu'l-Bahá

11 <u>Sh</u>araf   10 January

BLESSED is that teacher who remaineth faithful to the Covenant of God, and occupieth himself with the education of children. For him hath the Supreme Pen inscribed that reward which is revealed in the Most Holy Book.

Blessed, blessed is he!

Bahá'u'lláh

12 <u>Sh</u>araf   11 January

O YE that stand fast in the Covenant! When the hour cometh that this wronged and broken winged bird will have taken its flight unto the Celestial Concourse, when it will have hastened to the Realm of the Unseen, and its mortal frame will have either been lost or hidden neath the dust, it is incumbent upon the Afnán that are steadfast in the Covenant of God and have branched from the Tree of Holiness, the Hands of the Cause of God (the glory of the Lord rest upon them), and all the friends and loved ones, one and all, to bestir themselves and arise with heart and soul and in one accord to diffuse the sweet savours of God, to teach His Cause and to promote His Faith. It behooveth them not to rest for a moment, neither to seek repose. They must disperse themselves in every land, pass by every clime, and travel throughout all regions. Bestirred, without rest, and steadfast to the end, they must raise in every land the triumphal cry of Yá-Bahá'u'l-Abhá, must achieve renown in the world wherever they go, must burn brightly even as a candle in every meeting, and must kindle the flame of Divine Love in every assembly; that the Light of Truth may rise resplendent in the midmost heart of the world, that throughout the East and throughout the West a vast concourse may gather under the shadow of the Word of God, that the sweet savours of Holiness may be diffused, that faces may shine radiantly, hearts be filled with the Divine Spirit and souls be made heavenly.

'Abdu'l-Bahá

13 <u>Sharaf</u>   12 January

IN short, from these Holy Utterances and those of His Holiness Christ, it becomes clear, evident and proved, that man should associate with people who are firm in the Covenant and Testament, and befriend the pure ones; because bad associates bring about infection of bad qualities. It is like leprosy; it is impossible for a man to associate and befriend a leper and not be infected. This command is for the sake of protection and to safeguard.

'Abdu'l-Bahá

14 <u>Sharaf</u>   13 January

AFTER man's recognition of God, and becoming steadfast in His Cause, the station of affection, of harmony, of concord and of unity is superior to that of most other goodly deeds.

This is what He Who is the Desire of the world hath testified at every morn and eve. God grant that ye may follow that which hath been revealed in the Kitáb-i-Aqdas.

Bahá'u'lláh

15 <u>Sh</u>araf   14 January

GOD has not created men that they should destroy one another. All races, tribes, sects and classes share equally in the Bounty of their Heavenly Father.

The only difference lies in the degree of faithfulness, of obedience to the laws of God. There are some who are as lighted torches, there are others who shine as stars in the sky of humanity. The lovers of mankind, these are the superior men, of whatever nation, creed or colour they may be. For it is they to whom God will say these blessed words, 'Well done, My good and faithful servants.'

'Abdu'l-Bahá

16 <u>Sh</u>araf   15 January

THEY whom God hath endued with insight will readily recognize that the precepts laid down by God constitute the highest means for the maintenance of order in the world and the security of its peoples. He that turneth away from them, is accounted among the abject and foolish. We, verily, have commanded you to refuse the dictates of your evil passions and corrupt desires, and not to transgress the bounds which the Pen of the Most High hath fixed, for these are the breath of life unto all created things. The seas of Divine wisdom and divine utterance have risen under the breath of the breeze of the All-Merciful. Hasten to drink your fill, O men

181

of understanding! They that have violated the Covenant of
God by breaking His commandments, and have turned back
on their heels, these have erred grievously in the sight of
God, the All-Possessing, the Most High.

Bahá'u'lláh

17 <u>Sh</u>araf 16 January

THEREFORE, you must read the Tablets of Bahá'u'lláh. You
must read the Tablet of the Branch and regard that which
He has so clearly stated. Beware! Beware! lest anyone
should speak from the authority of his own thoughts or
create a new thing out of himself. Beware! Beware!
According to the explicit Covenant of Bahá'u'lláh you
should care nothing at all for such a person. Bahá'u'lláh
shuns such souls. I have expounded these things for you,
for the conservation and protection of the teachings of
Bahá'u'lláh, in order that you may be informed, lest any
souls shall deceive you and lest any souls shall cause
suspicion among you.

'Abdu'l-Bahá

18 <u>Sh</u>araf 17 January

IF the lovers of the Lord are hoping for grace to win as their
friends the Company on high, they must do all they can to
strengthen this compact, for such an alliance for brotherhood and unity is even as watering the Tree of Life: it is life
everlasting.

O ye lovers of God! Make firm your steps; fulfil your
pledge to one another; go forth in harmony to scatter abroad
the sweet savours of God's love, and to establish His

Teachings, until ye breathe a soul into the dead body of this world, and bring true healing in the physical and spiritual realms to everyone who aileth . . .

O ye lovers of God! Be kind to all peoples; care for every person; do all ye can to purify the hearts and minds of men; strive ye to gladden every soul. To every meadow be a shower of grace, to every tree the water of life; be as sweet musk to the sense of humankind, and to the ailing be a fresh, restoring breeze. Be pleasing waters to all those who thirst, a careful guide to all who have lost their way; be father and mother to the orphan, be loving sons and daughters to the old, be an abundant treasure to the poor. Think ye of love and good fellowship as the delights of heaven, think ye of hostility and hatred as the torments of hell . . .

See ye, therefore, to your own tasks: guide ye the people and educate them in the ways of 'Abdu'l-Bahá. Deliver to mankind this joyous message from the Abhá Realm. Rest not, by day or night; seek ye no moment's peace. Strive ye with all your might to bring to men's ears these happy tidings. In your love for God and your attachment to 'Abdu'l-Bahá, accept ye every tribulation, every sorrow. Endure the aggressor's taunts, put up with the enemy's reproaches. Follow in the footsteps of 'Abdu'l-Bahá, and in the pathway of the Abhá Beauty, long at every moment to give up your lives. Shine out like the day-star, be unresting as the sea; even as the clouds of heaven, shed ye life upon field and hill, and like unto April winds, blow freshness through those human trees, and bring them to their blossoming.

'Abdu'l-Bahá

19 *Sharaf*   *18 January*

O HOW I long to see the loved ones taking upon themselves

the responsibilities of the Cause! Now is the time to proclaim the Kingdom of Bahá! Now is the hour of love and union! This is the day of the spiritual harmony of the loved ones of God! All the resources of my physical strength I have exhausted, and the spirit of my life is the welcome tidings of the unity of the people of Bahá. I am straining my ears toward the East and toward the West, toward the North and toward the South that haply I may hear the songs of love and fellowship chanted in the meetings of the faithful. My days are numbered, and, but for this, there is no joy left unto me. O how I yearn to see the friends united even as a string of gleaming pearls, as the brilliant Pleiades, as the rays of the sun, as the gazelles of one meadow!

The mystic Nightingale is warbling for them all; will they not listen? The Bird of Paradise is singing; will they not heed? The Angel of Abhá is calling to them; will they not hearken? The Herald of the Covenant is pleading; will they not obey?

Ah me, I am waiting, waiting, to hear the joyful tidings that the believers are the very embodiment of sincerity and truthfulness, the incarnation of love and amity, the living symbols of unity and concord. Will they not gladden my heart? Will they not satisfy my yearning? Will they not manifest my wish? Will they not fulfil my heart's desire? Will they not give ear to my call?

I am waiting, I am patiently waiting.

'Abdu'l-Bahá

The month of Sultán begins at sunset.

17

Sulṭán
(Sovereignty)

Breaking the Covenant

Feast of Sulṭán

1 Sulṭán   19 January

THOU art the One, O my God and my Ruler, Who hast sent
down Thy Book that Thou mayest manifest my Cause, and
glorify my Word. Through it Thou didst enter into a
Covenant, concerning me, with all that hath been created in
Thy realm. Thou seest, O Beloved of the world, how the
rebellious among Thy creatures have made of that Covenant
a bulwark for themselves, and through it have withdrawn
from Thy Beauty, and repudiated Thy signs.

Bahá'u'lláh

2 Sulṭán   20 January

PRAISE be unto God Who hath manifested the Point, hath
unfolded therefrom the knowledge of all things, whether of
the past or of the future – a Point He hath chosen to be the
Herald of His Name and the Harbinger of His Great
Revelation which hath caused the limbs of all mankind to
quake and the splendour of His light to shine forth above the

horizon of the world. Verily, this is the Point which God hath ordained to be an ocean of light for the sincere among His servants and a flame of fire to the froward amidst His creatures and the impious among His people – they who bartered away the gift of God for unbelief, and the celestial food for hypocrisy, and led their associates to a wretched abode. These are the people who have manifested sedition throughout the world and have violated His Covenant on the Day when the immortal Being mounted His throne and the Crier raised His Voice from the haven of security and peace in the holy Vale.

Bahá'u'lláh

3 Sulṭán   21 January

ONE of the enemies of the Cause is he who endeavours to interpret the Words of Bahá'u'lláh and thereby colours the meaning according to his capacity, and collects around him a following, forming a different sect, promoting his own station, and making a division in the Cause.

'Abdu'l-Bahá

4 Sulṭán   22 January

AMONG the people are those who have broken the Covenant and among them are those who have followed what was ordained by the All-Knower, the All-Wise. My affliction is not from My imprisonment and persecution, or from what comes to Me from My rebellious servants – but from the actions of those who attribute themselves to this persecuted One and commit among the people that which is degrading to the honour of God. Verily, they are of the seditious.

Bahá'u'lláh

5 Sulṭán   23 January

IN short, according to the explicit Divine Text the least transgression shall make of this man a fallen creature, and what transgression is more grievous than attempting to destroy the Divine Edifice, breaking the Covenant, erring from the testament, falsifying the Holy Text, sowing the seeds of doubt, calumniating 'Abdu'l-Bahá, advancing claims for which God hath sent down no warrant, kindling mischief and striving to shed the very blood of 'Abdu'l-Bahá, and many other things whereof ye are all aware! It is thus evident that should this man succeed in bringing disruption into the Cause of God, he will utterly destroy and exterminate it. Beware lest ye approach this man, for to approach him is worse than approaching fire!

'Abdu'l-Bahá

6 Sulṭán   24 January

CALL ye to mind that covenant ye have entered into with Me upon Mount Paran, situate within the hallowed precincts of Zaman. I have taken to witness the concourse on high and the dwellers in the city of eternity, yet now none I do find faithful unto the covenant. Of a certainty pride and rebellion have effaced it from the hearts, in such wise that no trace thereof remaineth. Yet knowing this, I waited and disclosed it not.

Bahá'u'lláh

7 Sulṭán   25 January

THE Supreme Concourse will pray for the one who is

adorned with the garment of faithfulness between heaven and earth; but he who breaks the Covenant is cursed by heaven and earth.

Bahá'u'lláh

8 Sulṭán   26 January

THOSE who have broken the Covenant of God, notwithstanding His Commands, and have turned away, they are the people of error before the most Opulent, the Exalted.

Bahá'u'lláh

9 Sulṭán   27 January

NOW some of the mischief-makers, with many stratagems, are seeking leadership, and in order to reach this position they instil doubts among the friends that they may cause differences, and that these differences may result in their drawing a party to themselves. But the friends of God must be awake and must know that the scattering of these doubts hath as its motive personal desires and the achievement of leadership.

'Abdu'l-Bahá

10 Sulṭán   28 January

AND now, one of the greatest and most fundamental principles of the Cause of God is to shun and avoid entirely the Covenant-breakers, for they will utterly destroy the Cause of God, exterminate His Law and render of no account all efforts exerted in the past. O friends! It behoveth you to call to mind with tenderness the trials of His Holiness, the Exalted One, and show your fidelity to the Ever-Blest Beauty. The utmost endeavour must be exerted lest all these woes, trials, and afflictions, all this pure and sacred blood that hath been shed so profusely in the Path of God, may prove to be in vain.

O ye beloved of the Lord! Strive with all your heart to shield the Cause of God from the onslaught of the insincere, for souls such as these cause the straight to become crooked and all benevolent efforts to produce contrary results.

O God! my God! I call Thee, Thy Prophets and Thy Messengers, Thy Saints and Thy Holy Ones, to witness that I have declared conclusively Thy Proofs unto Thy loved ones and set forth clearly all things unto them, that they may watch over Thy Faith, guard Thy Straight Path, and protect Thy Resplendent Law. Thou art, verily, the All-Knowing, the All-Wise!

'Abdu'l-Bahá

11 Sulṭán   29 January

IN all His Books and Tablets He has praised those who are firm in the Covenant and rebuked those who are not. He said, 'Verily, shun those who are shaken in the Covenant. Verily, God is the Confirmer of the firm ones.' In His prayers He has said, 'O God! Render those who are firm in the Covenant blessed, and degrade those who are not. O God! Be the Protector of him who protecteth Him, and confirm him who confirms the Centre of the Covenant.' Many utterances are directed against the violators of the Covenant, the purpose being that no dissension should arise in the blessed Cause; that no one should say, 'My opinion is this'; and that all may know Who is the authoritative expounder and whatsoever He says is correct. Bahá'u'lláh has not left any possible room for dissension.

'Abdu'l-Bahá

12 Sulṭán   30 January

A HUNDRED times it hath been foretold that the violators are lying in ambush and by every means desire to cause dissension among the friends so that this dissension may end in violation of the Covenant. How is it that, notwithstanding this warning, the friends have ignored this explicit statement?

The point at issue is clear, direct, and of the utmost brevity. Either Bahá'u'lláh was wise, omniscient and aware of what would ensue, or was ignorant and in error.

. . . One must say that the Blessed Beauty hath made a mistake or He must be obeyed.

'Abdu'l-Bahá

13 Sulṭán   31 January

THOU hadst asked some questions; that why the blessed and spiritual souls, who are firm and steadfast, shun the company of degenerate persons. This is because, that just as bodily diseases . . . are contagious, likewise the spiritual diseases are also infectious. If a consumptive should associate with a thousand safe and healthy persons, the safety and health of these thousand persons would not affect the consumptive and would not cure him of his consumption. But when this consumptive associates with those thousand souls, in a short time the disease of consumption will infect a number of those healthy persons. This is a clear and self-evident question.

'Abdu'l-Bahá

14 Sulṭán   1 February

BAHÁ'U'LLÁH, in all the Tablets and Epistles, forbade the true and firm friends from associating and meeting the violators of the Covenant of His Holiness the Báb, saying that no one should go near them because their breath is like the poison of the snake that kills instantly.

'Abdu'l-Bahá

15 Sulṭán   2 February

MY purpose is, however, to show that it is incumbent upon the friends that are fast and firm in the Covenant and Testament to be ever wakeful lest after this wronged one is gone this alert and active worker of mischief may cause disruption, privily sow the seeds of doubt and sedition, and utterly root out the Cause of God. A thousand times shun his company. Take heed and be on your guard. Watch and examine; should anyone, openly or privily, have the least connection with him cast him out from your midst, for he will surely cause disruption and mischief.

O ye beloved of the Lord! Strive with all your heart to shield the Cause of God from the onslaught of the insincere, for souls such as these cause the straight to become crooked and all benevolent efforts to produce contrary results.

'Abdu'l-Bahá

16 Sulṭán   3 February

ENDEAVOUR to your utmost to protect yourselves, because satan appears in different robes and appeals to everyone according to each person's own way, until he becomes like unto him (satan), then he will leave him alone . . . Be informed by these utterances and shun the manifestations of the people of hell . . . The greatest of degradation is to leave the Shadow of God and enter under the shadow of satan.

Bahá'u'lláh

17 Sulṭán   4 February

THOU hast written that in view of the questions of violation thou art perturbed. There is no occasion for perturbation for the Blessed Beauty (Bahá'u'lláh) has closed all doors of error and doubt and has entered with all the friends into a Covenant and a Testament.

'Abdu'l-Bahá

18 Sulṭán   5 February

TAKE hold of what has been revealed unto you, with a power superior to that of the hands of the unbelievers who have violated the Covenant of God and His Testament, and have turned from the Face.

Bahá'u'lláh

19 Sulṭán   6 February

VERILY, 'Abdu'l-Bahá inhaleth the fragrance of the love

of God from every meeting-place where the Word of God is uttered, and proofs and arguments set forth, that shed their rays across the world; and where they recount the tribulations of 'Abdu'l-Bahá at the evil hands of those who have violated the Covenant of God.

'Abdu'l-Bahá

The month of Mulk begins at sunset.

18

Mulk
(Dominion)

Opposition to the Cause

Feast of Mulk

1 Mulk   *7 February*

SHOULD you acquaint yourself with the indignities heaped upon the Prophets of God, and apprehend the true causes of the objections voiced by their oppressors, you will surely appreciate the significance of their position. Moreover, the more closely you observe the denials of those who have opposed the Manifestations of the divine attributes, the firmer will be your faith in the Cause of God.

Bahá'u'lláh

2 Mulk   *8 February*

O THOU Remnant of God! I have sacrificed myself wholly for Thee; I have accepted curses for Thy sake, and have yearned for naught but martyrdom in the path of Thy Love. Sufficient witness unto me is God, the Exalted, the Protector, the Ancient of Days.

The Báb

3 Mulk   9 February

WARN, O Salmán, the beloved of the one true God, not to
view with too critical an eye the sayings and writings of men.
Let them rather approach such sayings and writings in a
spirit of open-mindedness and loving sympathy. Those men,
however, who, in this Day, have been led to assail, in their
inflammatory writings, the tenets of the Cause of God, are
to be treated differently. It is incumbent upon all men, each
according to his ability, to refute the arguments of those that
have attacked the Faith of God. Thus hath it been decreed
by Him Who is the All-Powerful, the Almighty.

Bahá'u'lláh

4 Mulk   10 February

THE Hand of Omnipotence hath established His Revelation
upon an unassailable, an enduring foundation. Storms of
human strife are powerless to undermine its basis, nor will
men's fanciful theories succeed in damaging its structure.

Bahá'u'lláh

5 Mulk   11 February

SAY: O people of God! Beware lest the powers of the earth
alarm you, or the might of the nations weaken you, or the
tumult of the people of discord deter you, or the exponents
of earthly glory sadden you. Be ye as a mountain in the
Cause of your Lord, the Almighty, the All-Glorious, the
Unconstrained.

Bahá'u'lláh

6 Mulk   12 February

ALL who arise to serve the Cause of God will be persecuted
and misunderstood. It hath ever been so, and will ever be.
Let neither enemy nor friend disturb your composure,
destroy your happiness, deter your accomplishment. Rely
wholly upon God. Then will persecution and slander make
you the more radiant. The designs of your enemies will
rebound upon them. They, not you, will suffer. Oppression
is the wind that doth fan the fire of the Love of God.
Welcome persecution and bitterness. A soldier may bear
arms, but until he hath faced the enemy in battle he hath not
earned his place in the king's army. Let nothing defeat you.
God is your helper. God is invincible. Be firm in the
Heavenly Covenant. Pray for strength. It will be given to
you, no matter how difficult the conditions.

'Abdu'l-Bahá

7 Mulk   13 February

HOW great, how very great is the Cause! How very fierce the
onslaught of all the peoples and kindreds of the earth . . .
One and all, they shall arise with all their power to resist His
Cause. Then shall the knights of the Lord, assisted by His
grace from on high, strengthened by faith, aided by the
power of understanding, and reinforced by the legions of the
Covenant, arise and make manifest the truth of the verse:
'Behold the confusion that hath befallen the tribes of the
defeated!'

'Abdu'l-Bahá

8 Mulk   14 February

THE tests of every dispensation are in direct proportion to

the greatness of the Cause and as heretofore such a manifest Covenant, written by the Supreme Pen, has not been entered upon, the tests are proportionately severe.

'Abdu'l-Bahá

9 Mulk   15 February

. . . some people may arise in opposition, heaping persecutions upon you in their bitterness, and in the newspapers there may be articles published against the Cause. Rest ye in the assurance of firmness. Be well poised and serene, remembering that this is only as the harmless twittering of sparrows and that it will soon pass away . . . Therefore, my purpose is to warn and strengthen you against accusations, criticisms, revilings and derision in newspaper articles or other publications. Be not disturbed by them. They are the very confirmation of the Cause, the very source of upbuilding to the Movement. May God confirm the day when a score of ministers of the churches may arise and with bared heads cry at the top of their voices that the Bahá'ís are misguided. I would like to see that day, for that is the time when the Cause of God will spread. Bahá'u'lláh has pronounced such as these the couriers of the Cause. They will proclaim from pulpits that the Bahá'ís are fools, that they are a wicked and unrighteous people, but be ye steadfast and unwavering in the Cause of God. They will spread the message of Bahá'u'lláh.

'Abdu'l-Bahá

10 Mulk   16 February

. . . a large multitude of people will arise against you,

showing oppression, expressing contumely and derision, shunning your society, and heaping upon you ridicule. However, the Heavenly Father will illumine you to such an extent that, like unto the rays of the sun, you shall scatter the dark clouds of superstition, shine gloriously in the midst of Heaven and illumine the face of the earth. You must make firm the feet at the time when these trials transpire, and demonstrate forbearance and patience. You must withstand them with the utmost love and kindness; consider their oppression and persecution as the caprice of children, and do not give any importance to whatever they do. For at the end the illumination of the Kingdom will overwhelm the darkness of the world and the exaltation and grandeur of your station will become apparent and manifest . . .

'Abdu'l-Bahá

11 Mulk   17 February

O YE beloved of God! When the winds blow severely, rains fall fiercely, the lightning flashes, the thunder roars, the bolt descends and storms of trial become severe, grieve not; for after this storm, verily, the divine spring will arrive, the hills and fields will become verdant, the expanses of grain will joyfully wave, the earth will become covered with blossoms, the trees will be clothed with green garments and adorned with blossoms and fruits. Thus blessings become manifest in all countries. These favours are results of those storms and hurricanes . . .

Therefore, O ye beloved of God, be not grieved when people stand against you, persecute you, afflict and trouble you and say all manner of evil against you. The darkness will pass away and the light of the manifest signs will appear, the veil will be withdrawn and the Light of Reality will shine forth from the unseen (Kingdom) of El-Abhá. This we inform you before it occurs, so that when the hosts of people arise against you for my love, be not disturbed or troubled; nay rather, be firm as a mountain, for this persecution and reviling of the people upon you is a pre-ordained matter. Blessed is the soul who is firm in the path!

'Abdu'l-Bahá

12 Mulk   18 February

O ARMY of God! When calamity striketh, be ye patient and composed. However afflictive your sufferings may be, stay ye undisturbed, and with perfect confidence in the abounding grace of God, brave ye the tempest of tribulations and fiery ordeals.

'Abdu'l-Bahá

13 Mulk   19 February

O YE loved ones of God! From the peoples of the world, against the Candle of the Covenant discordant winds do beat and blow. The Nightingale of faithfulness is beset by renegades who are even as ravens of hate. The Dove of God's remembrance is hard pressed by mindless birds of night, and the Gazelle that dwelleth in the meadows of God's love is being hunted down by ravening beasts. Deadly is the peril, tormenting the pain.

The beloved of the Lord must stand fixed as the mountains, firm as impregnable walls. Unmoved must they remain by even the direst adversities, ungrieved by the worst of disasters. Let them cling to the hem of Almighty God, and put their faith in the Beauty of the Most High; let them lean on the unfailing help that cometh from the Ancient Kingdom, and depend on the care and protection of the generous Lord. Let them at all times refresh and restore themselves with the dews of heavenly grace, and with the breaths of the Holy Spirit revive and renew themselves from moment to moment. Let them rise up to serve their Lord, and do all in their power to scatter His breathings of holiness far and wide. Let them be a mighty fortress to defend His Faith, an impregnable citadel for the hosts of the Ancient Beauty. Let them faithfully guard the edifice of the Cause of God from every side; let them become the bright stars of His luminous skies. For the hordes of darkness are assailing this Cause from every direction, and the peoples of the earth are intent on extinguishing this evident Light. And since all the kindreds of the world are mounting their attack, how can our attention be diverted, even for a moment? Assuredly be cognizant of these things, be watchful, and guard the Cause of God.

'Abdu'l-Bahá

14 Mulk   20 February

YOU should exhort all the friends to patience, to acquiescence, and to tranquillity, saying: O ye loved ones of God in that land! Ye are glorified in all the worlds of God because of your relationship to Him Who is the Eternal Truth, but in your lives on this earthly plane, which pass away as a fleeting moment, ye are afflicted with abasement. For the sake of the one true God, ye have been reviled and persecuted, ye have been imprisoned, and surrendered your lives in His path. Ye should not, however, by reason of the tyrannical acts of some heedless souls, transgress the limits of God's commandments by contending with anyone.

Whatever hath befallen you, hath been for the sake of

God. This is the truth, and in this there is no doubt. You should, therefore, leave all your affairs in His Hands, place your trust in Him, and rely upon Him. He will assuredly not forsake you. In this, likewise, there is no doubt. No father will surrender his sons to devouring beasts; no shepherd will leave his flock to ravening wolves. He will most certainly do his utmost to protect his own.

Bahá'u'lláh

15 Mulk   21 February

AND likewise, He saith: 'Say to them that are of a fearful heart: be strong, fear not, behold your God.' This blessed verse is a proof of the greatness of the Revelation, and of the greatness of the Cause, inasmuch as the blast of the trumpet must needs spread confusion throughout the world, and fear and trembling amongst all men. Well is it with him who hath been illumined with the light of trust and detachment. The tribulations of that Day will not hinder or alarm him. Thus hath the Tongue of Utterance spoken, as bidden by Him Who is the All-Merciful. He, verily, is the Strong, the All-Powerful, the All-Subduing, the Almighty.

Bahá'u'lláh

16 Mulk   22 February

O THOU who has been sore afflicted on the pathway of the Covenant! Anguish and torment, when suffered on the pathway of the Lord, Him of manifest signs, is only favour and grace; affliction is but mercy, and grief a gift from God. Poison is sugar on the tongue, and wrath is kindness, nourishing the soul.

'Abdu'l-Bahá

17 Mulk   23 February

IN these days the Cause of God, the world over, is fast growing in power and, day by day, is spreading further and further to the utmost bounds of the earth. Its enemies, therefore, from all the kindreds and peoples of the world, are growing aggressive, malevolent, envious and bitterly hostile. It is incumbent upon the loved ones of God to exercise the greatest care and prudence in all things, whether great or small, to take counsel together and unitedly resist the onslaught of the stirrers up of strife and the movers of mischief.

'Abdu'l-Bahá

18 Mulk   24 February

WHEN the victory arriveth, every man shall profess himself as a believer and shall hasten to the shelter of God's Faith. Happy are they who in the days of world-encompassing trials have stood fast in the Cause and refused to swerve from its truth.

Bahá'u'lláh

19 Mulk   25 February

O GOD, my God! Lowly, suppliant, and fallen upon my face, I beseech Thee with all the ardour of my invocation to pardon whosoever hath hurt me, forgive him that hath conspired against me and offended me, and wash away the misdeeds of them that have wrought injustice upon me. Vouchsafe unto them Thy goodly gifts, give them joy, relieve them from sorrow, grant them peace and prosperity, give them Thy bliss and pour upon them Thy bounty.

Thou art the Powerful, the Gracious, the Help in Peril, the Self-Subsisting!

'Abdu'l-Bahá

The celebration of Ayyám-i-Há begins at sunset.

Ayyám-i-Há
(Intercalary Days)

The Joy of Firmness in the Covenant

Ayyám-i-Há   *26 February*

IF thou truly givest ear to that which hath been revealed for thee from My Supreme Pen at this moment, thou shalt soar with the wings of eagerness in the heaven of love for the Lord of the Day of the Covenant, and wilt say during all the days of thy life: Thanks be unto Thee, O Thou the Desire of the world, and praise be unto Thee, O Thou the Beloved of the people of understanding. May all existence be a sacrifice for Thy favour, and all that hath been and will ever be, a ransom for Thy Word, O Thou the Wronged One amongst the people of enmity, O Thou in Whose grasp are the reins of all who are in heaven and on earth . . .

Bahá'u'lláh

Ayyám-i-Há   *27 February*

O YE who are holding fast unto the Covenant and Testament! This day, from the realms of the All-Glorious, from the Kingdom of Holiness where hosannas of glorification and praise rise up, the Company on high direct their gaze upon you. Whensoever their gaze lighteth upon gatherings of those who are steadfast in the Covenant and Testament, then do they utter their cry, 'Glad tidings! Glad tidings!' Then, exulting, do they lift up their voices, and shout, 'O ye spiritual communion! O ye gathering of God! Blessed are ye! Glad tidings be unto you! Bright be your faces, and be ye of good cheer, for ye cling to the Covenant of the Beloved of all the worlds, ye are on fire with the wine of His Testament. Ye have plighted your troth to the Ancient of Days, ye have drunk deep from the chalice of loyalty. Ye have guarded and defended the Cause of God; ye have not been a cause of dividing up His Word; ye have not brought His Faith low, but have striven to glorify His Holy Name; ye have not allowed the Blessed Cause to be exposed to the derision of the people. Ye have not permitted the Designated Station to be humbled, nor been willing to see the Centre of Authority discredited or exposed to mockery and persecution. Ye have striven to keep the Word whole and one. Ye have passed through the portals of mercy. Ye have not let the Blessed Beauty slip from your minds, to fade unremembered.'

The Glory rest upon you.

'Abdu'l-Bahá

Ayyám-i-Há   28 February

O YE loved ones of God! The wine-cup of Heaven overfloweth, the banquet of God's Covenant is bright with festive lights, the dawn of all bestowals is breaking, the gentle winds of grace are blowing, and out of the invisible world come good tidings of bounties and gifts. In flower-spangled meadows hath the divine springtime pitched its tents, and the spiritual are inhaling sweet scents from the Sheba of the spirit, carried their way by the east wind. Now doth the mystic nightingale carol its odes, and buds of inner

meaning are bursting into blossoms delicate and fair. The
field larks are become the festival's musicians, and lifting
wondrous voices they cry and sing to the melodies of the
Company on high, 'Blessed are ye! Glad Tidings! Glad
Tidings!' And they urge on the revellers of the Abhá
Paradise to drink their fill, and they eloquently hold forth
upon the celestial tree, and utter their sacred cries. All this,
that withered souls who tread the desert of the heedless, and
faded ones lost in the sands of unconcern, may come to
throbbing life again, and present themselves at the feasts
and revels of the Lord God.

'Abdu'l-Bahá

Ayyám-i-Há   29 February

ARISE with every power to assist the Covenant of God and
serve in His vineyard. Be confident that a confirmation will
be granted unto you and a success on His part is given unto
you. Verily, He shall support you by the angels of His
holiness and reinforce you with the breaths of the Spirit that
ye may mount the Ark of Safety, set forth the evident signs,
impart the spirit of life, declare the essence of His
commands and precepts, guide the sheep who are straying
from the fold in all directions, and give the blessings. Ye
have to use every effort in your power and strive earnestly
and wisely in this new century. By God, verily the Lord of
Hosts is your support, the angels of heaven your assistance,
the Holy Spirit your companion and the Centre of the
Covenant your helper. Be not idle, but active and fear not.
Look unto those who have been in the former ages – how
they have resisted all nations and suffered all persecutions
and afflictions, and how their stars shone, their attacks
proved successful, their teachings established, their regions

expanded, their hearts gladdened, their ideas cleared and their motives effective. Ye are now in a great station and noble rank and ye shall find yourselves in evident success and prosperity, the like of which the eye of existence never saw in former ages.

'Abdu'l-Bahá

Ayyám-i-Há *1 March*

IF you observe that a soul has turned his face completely toward the Cause of God, his intention is centralized upon the penetration of the Word of God, he is serving the Cause day and night with the utmost fidelity, no scent of selfishness is inhaled from his manners and deeds, and no trace of egotism or prejudice is seen in his personality – nay rather is he a wanderer in the wilderness of the love of God, and one intoxicated with the wine of the knowledge of God, occupied wholly with the diffusion of the fragrances of God, and attracted to the signs of the Kingdom of God; know ye of a certainty that he is confirmed with the powers of the Kingdom, assisted by the heaven of might; and he will shine, gleam, and sparkle like unto the morning star with the utmost brilliancy and splendour from the horizon of the everlasting gift.

'Abdu'l-Bahá

The month of 'Alá and the Fast begin at sunset.

19

'Alá
(Loftiness)

Prayers for Firmness in the Covenant

The Fast
The Feast of 'Alá

1 'Alá   2 March

I BESEECH Thee, by Thy Most Great Name, to open the eyes of Thy servants, that they may behold Thee shining above the horizon of Thy majesty and glory, and that they may not be hindered by the croaking of the raven from hearkening to the voice of the Dove of Thy sublime oneness, nor be prevented by the corrupt waters from partaking of the pure wine of Thy bounty and the everlasting streams of Thy gifts.

Gather them, then, together around this Divine Law, the covenant of which Thou hast established with all Thy Prophets and Thy Messengers, and Whose ordinances Thou hast written down in Thy Tablets and Thy Scriptures. Raise them up, moreover, to such heights as will enable them to perceive Thy Call.

Potent art Thou to do what pleaseth Thee. Thou art, verily, the Inaccessible, the All-Glorious.

Bahá'u'lláh

2 'Alá   3 March

PRAISE be to Thee, O Lord, my Best Beloved! Make me

steadfast in Thy Cause and grant that I may be reckoned among those who have not violated Thy Covenant nor followed the gods of their own idle fancy. Enable me, then, to obtain a seat of truth in Thy presence, bestow upon me a token of Thy mercy and let me join with such of Thy servants as shall have no fear nor shall they be put to grief.

The Báb

3 'Alá   *4 March*

GLORIFIED art Thou, O Lord my God! I pray Thee, by Him Who is the Day-Spring of Thy signs and the Manifestation of Thy names, and the Treasury of Thine inspiration, and the Repository of Thy wisdom, to send upon Thy loved ones that which will enable them to cleave steadfastly to Thy Cause, and to recognize Thy unity, and to acknowledge Thy oneness, and to bear witness to Thy divinity. Raise them up, O my God, to such heights that they will recognize in all things the tokens of the power of Him Who is the Manifestation of Thy most august and all-glorious Self.

Thou art He, O my Lord, Who doeth what He willeth, and ordaineth what He pleaseth. Every possessor of power is forlorn before the revelations of Thy might, and every fountain of honour becomes abject when confronted by the manifold evidences of Thy great glory.

I beseech Thee, by Thyself and by whatsoever is of Thee, to grant that I may help Thy Cause and speak of Thy praise, and set my heart on the sanctuary of Thy glory, and detach myself from all that pertaineth not unto Thee. No God is there beside Thee, the God of power, the God of glory and wisdom.

Bahá'u'lláh

4 'Alá   5 March

O COMPASSIONATE God! Thanks be to Thee for Thou hast awakened and made me conscious. Thou hast given me a seeing eye and favoured me with a hearing ear, hast led me to Thy kingdom and guided me to Thy path. Thou hast shown me the right way and caused me to enter the ark of deliverance. O God! Keep me steadfast and make me firm and staunch. Protect me from violent tests, and preserve and shelter me in the strongly fortified fortress of Thy Covenant and Testament. Thou art the Powerful. Thou art the Seeing. Thou art the Hearing.

O Thou the Compassionate God. Bestow upon me a heart which, like unto a glass, may be illumined with the light of Thy love, and confer upon me thoughts which may change this world into a rose garden through the outpourings of heavenly grace.

Thou art the Compassionate, the Merciful. Thou art the Great Beneficent God.

'Abdu'l-Bahá

5 'Alá   6 March

O THOU Whose nearness is my wish, Whose presence is my hope, Whose remembrance is my desire, Whose court of glory is my goal, Whose abode is my aim, Whose name is my healing, Whose love is the radiance of my heart, Whose service is my highest aspiration! I beseech Thee by Thy Name, through which Thou hast enabled them that have recognized Thee to soar to the sublimest heights of the knowledge of Thee and empowered such as devoutly worship Thee to ascend into the precincts of the court of Thy holy favours, to aid me to turn my face toward Thy face, to fix mine eyes upon Thee, and to speak of Thy glory.

I am the one, O my Lord, who hath forgotten all else but Thee, and turned towards the Day-Spring of Thy grace, who hath forsaken all save Thyself in the hope of drawing nigh unto Thy court. Behold me, then, with mine eyes lifted up towards the Seat that shineth with the splendours of the light of Thy Face. Send down, then, upon me, O my Beloved, that which will enable me to be steadfast in Thy Cause, so that the doubts of the infidels may not hinder me from turning towards Thee.

Thou art, verily, the God of Power, the Help in Peril, the All-Glorious, the Almighty.

Bahá'u'lláh

6 'Alá   7 March

O MY Lord and my Hope! Help Thou Thy loved ones to be steadfast in Thy mighty Covenant, to remain faithful to Thy manifest Cause, and to carry out the commandments Thou didst set down for them in Thy Book of Splendours; that they may become banners of guidance and lamps of the Company above, wellsprings of Thine infinite wisdom, and stars that lead aright, as they shine down from the supernal sky.

Verily art Thou the Invincible, the Almighty, the All-Powerful.

'Abdu'l-Bahá

7 'Alá   8 March

HE is the Mighty, the Pardoner, the Compassionate!

O God, my God! Thou beholdest Thy servants in the abyss of perdition and error; where is Thy light of divine guidance, O Thou the Desire of the world? Thou knowest their helplessness and their feebleness; where is Thy power, O Thou in Whose grasp lie the powers of heaven and earth?

I ask Thee, O Lord my God, by the splendour of the lights of Thy loving-kindness and the billows of the ocean of Thy knowledge and wisdom and by Thy Word wherewith Thou hast swayed the peoples of Thy dominion, to grant that I may be one of them that have observed Thy bidding in Thy Book. And do Thou ordain for me that which Thou hast ordained for Thy trusted ones, them that have quaffed the wine of divine inspiration from the chalice of Thy bounty and hastened to do Thy pleasure and observe Thy Covenant and Testament. Powerful art Thou to do as Thou willest. There is none other God but Thee, the All-Knowing, the All-Wise.

Decree for me, by Thy bounty, O Lord, that which shall prosper me in this world and hereafter and shall draw me nigh unto Thee, O Thou Who art the Lord of all men. There is none other God but Thee, the One, the Mighty, the Glorified.

Bahá'u'lláh

8 'Alá   9 March

MAKE firm our steps, O Lord, in Thy path and strengthen Thou our hearts in Thine obedience. Turn our faces toward the beauty of Thy oneness, and gladden our bosoms with the signs of Thy divine unity. Adorn our bodies with the robe of Thy bounty, and remove from our eyes the veil of sinfulness, and give us the chalice of Thy grace; that the essence of all beings may sing Thy praise before the vision of Thy grandeur. Reveal then Thyself, O Lord, by Thy merciful utterance and the mystery of Thy divine being, that the holy ecstasy of prayer may fill our souls – a prayer that shall rise above words and letters and transcend the murmur of syllables and sounds – that all things may be merged into nothingness before the revelation of Thy splendour.

Lord! These are servants that have remained fast and firm in Thy Covenant and Thy Testament, that have held fast unto the cord of constancy in Thy Cause and clung unto the hem of the robe of Thy grandeur. Assist them, O Lord, with Thy grace, confirm with Thy power and strengthen their loins in obedience to Thee.

Thou art the Pardoner, the Gracious.

‘Abdu’l-Bahá

9 ‘Alá   10 March

GLORY be to Thee, O King of eternity, and the Maker of nations, and the Fashioner of every mouldering bone! I pray Thee, by Thy Name through which Thou didst call all mankind unto the horizon of Thy majesty and glory, and didst guide Thy servants to the court of Thy grace and favours, to number me with such as have rid themselves from everything except Thyself, and have set themselves towards Thee, and have not been kept back by such misfortunes as were decreed by Thee, from turning in the direction of Thy gifts.

I have laid hold, O my Lord, on the handle of Thy bounty, and clung steadfastly to the hem of the robe of Thy favour. Send down, then, upon me, out of the clouds of Thy generosity, what will purge out from me the remembrance of anyone except Thee, and make me able to turn unto Him Who is the Object of the adoration of all mankind, against Whom have been arrayed the stirrers of sedition, who have broken Thy covenant, and disbelieved in Thee and in Thy signs.

Deny me not, O my Lord, the fragrances of Thy raiment in Thy days, and deprive me not of the breathings of Thy Revelation at the appearance of the splendours of the light of Thy face. Powerful art Thou to do what pleaseth Thee. Naught can resist Thy will, nor frustrate what Thou hast purposed by Thy power.

No God is there but Thee, the Almighty, the All-Wise.

Bahá'u'lláh

10 'Alá   11 March

O LORD, my God! Assist Thy loved ones to be firm in Thy Faith, to walk in Thy ways, to be steadfast in Thy Cause. Give them Thy grace to withstand the onslaught of self and passion, to follow the light of Divine Guidance. Thou art the Powerful, the Gracious, the Self-Subsisting, the Bestower, the Compassionate, the All-Mighty, the All-Bountiful.

'Abdu'l-Bahá

11 'Alá   12 March

GLORIFIED art Thou, O Lord my God! I beseech Thee by Him Who is Thy Most Great Name, Who hath been sorely afflicted by such of Thy creatures as have repudiated Thy truth, and Who hath been hemmed in by sorrows which no tongue can describe, to grant that I may remember Thee and celebrate Thy praise, in these days when all have turned away from Thy beauty, have disputed with Thee, and turned away disdainfully from Him Who is the Revealer of Thy Cause. None is there, O my Lord, to help Thee except Thine own Self, and no power to succour Thee save Thine own power.

I entreat Thee to enable me to cleave steadfastly to Thy love and Thy remembrance. This is, verily, within my power, and Thou art the One that knoweth all that is in me. Thou, in truth, art knowing, apprised of all. Deprive me not, O my Lord, of the splendours of the light of Thy face, whose brightness hath illuminated the whole world. No God is there beside Thee, the Most Powerful, the All-Glorious, the Ever-Forgiving.

Bahá'u'lláh

12 'Alá   13 March

O GOD! Assist me with the hosts of the Supreme Concourse, and make me firm and steadfast in the Covenant and Testament. I am weak in the Covenant and Testament, confer upon me strength. I am poor, bestow upon me wealth from the treasury of the Kingdom. I am ignorant, open before my face the doors of knowledge. I am dead, breathe into me the breath of life. I am dumb, grant me an eloquent tongue, so that with a fluent expression I may raise the Call of Thy Kingdom and guide all to firmness in thy Covenant. Thou art the Generous, the Giver, and the Mighty.

'Abdu'l-Bahá

13 'Alá   14 March

O THOU Whose tests are a healing medicine to such as are nigh unto Thee, Whose sword is the ardent desire of all them that love Thee, Whose dart is the dearest wish of those hearts that yearn after Thee, Whose decree is the sole hope of them that have recognized Thy truth! I implore Thee, by Thy divine sweetness and by the splendours of the glory of Thy face, to send down upon us from Thy retreats on high that which will enable us to draw nigh unto Thee. Set, then, our feet firm, O my God, in Thy Cause, and enlighten our hearts with the effulgence of Thy knowledge, and illumine our breasts with the brightness of Thy names.

Bahá'u'lláh

14 'Alá   15 March

HE IS GOD!

O Lord, my God, my Well-Beloved! These are servants of Thine that have heard Thy Voice, given ear to Thy Word and hearkened to Thy Call. They have believed in Thee, witnessed Thy wonders, acknowledged Thy proof and testified to Thine evidence. They have walked in Thy ways, followed Thy guidance, discovered Thy mysteries, comprehended the secrets of Thy Book, the verses of Thy Scrolls and the tidings of Thy Epistles and Tablets. They have clung to the hem of Thy garment and held fast unto the robe of Thy light and grandeur. Their footsteps have been strengthened in Thy Covenant and their hearts made firm in Thy Testament. Lord! Do Thou kindle in their hearts the flame of Thy divine attraction and grant that the bird of love and understanding may sing within their hearts. Grant that they may be even as potent signs, resplendent standards, and perfect as Thy Word. Exalt by them Thy Cause, unfurl Thy banners and publish far and wide Thy wonders. Make by them Thy Word triumphant and strengthen the loins of Thy loved ones. Unloose their tongues to laud Thy Name and inspire them to do Thy holy will and pleasure. Illumine their faces in Thy Kingdom of holiness and perfect their joy by aiding them to arise for the triumph of Thy Cause.

Lord! Feeble are we, strengthen us to diffuse the fragrances of Thy Holiness; poor, enrich us from the treasures of Thy Divine Unity; naked, clothe us with the robe of Thy bounty; sinful, forgive us our sins by Thy grace, Thy favour and Thy pardon. Thou art verily the Aider, the Helper, the Gracious, the Mighty, the Powerful.

The glory of glories rest upon them that are fast and firm.

'Abdu'l-Bahá

15 'Alá   16 March

WE pray to God to graciously assist them that have been led astray to be just and fair-minded, and to make them aware of that whereof they have been heedless. He, in truth, is the All-Bounteous, the Most Generous. Debar not Thy servants, O my Lord, from the door of Thy grace, and drive them not away from the court of Thy presence. Assist them to dispel the mists of idle fancy, and to tear away the veils of vain imaginings and hopes. Thou art, verily, the All-Possessing, the Most High. No God is there but Thee, the Almighty, the Gracious.

Bahá'u'lláh

16 'Alá   17 March

HE is the Compassionate, the All-Bountiful! O God, my God! Thou seest me, Thou knowest me; Thou art my Haven and my Refuge. None have I sought nor any will I seek save Thee; no path have I trodden nor any will I tread but the path of Thy love. In the darksome night of despair, my eye turneth expectant and full of hope to the morn of Thy boundless favour, and at the hour of dawn my drooping soul is refreshed and strengthened in remembrance of Thy beauty and perfection. He whom the grace of Thy mercy aideth, though he be but a drop, shall become the boundless ocean, and the merest atom which the outpouring of Thy loving-kindness assisteth shall shine even as the radiant star.

Shelter under Thy protection, O Thou Spirit of Purity, Thou Who art the All-Bountiful Provider, this enthralled, enkindled servant of Thine. Aid him in this world of being to remain steadfast and firm in Thy love and grant that this broken-winged bird may attain a refuge and shelter in Thy Divine Nest, that abideth upon the Celestial Tree.

'Abdu'l-Bahá

17 *'Alá*　　　　　　　　　*18 March*

OUR limbs, our members, O my Lord, bear witness to Thy unity and oneness. Send down upon us Thy strength and power, that we may become steadfast in Thy Faith and may aid Thee among Thy servants. Illumine our eyes, O my Lord, with the effulgence of Thy beauty, and enlighten our hearts with the splendours of Thy knowledge and wisdom. Write us up, then, with those who have fulfilled their pledge to Thy Covenant in Thy days, and who, through their love for Thee, have detached themselves from the world and all that is therein.

Powerful art Thou to do what Thou pleasest. No God is there beside Thee, the All-Powerful, the Omniscient, the Supreme Ruler, the Help in Peril, the Self-Subsisting.

Bahá'u'lláh

18 *'Alá*　　　　　　　　　*19 March*

O THOU compassionate Lord! Thou Who art generous and

able! We are servants of Thine, sheltered beneath Thy providence. Cast Thy glance of favour upon us. Give light to our eyes, hearing to our ears, and understanding and love to our hearts. Render our souls joyous and happy through Thy glad-tidings. O Lord! Point out to us the pathway of Thy kingdom, and resuscitate all of us through the breaths of the Holy Spirit. Bestow upon us life everlasting and confer upon us never-ending honour. Unify mankind and illumine the world of humanity. May we all follow Thy pathway, long for Thy good-pleasure, and seek the mysteries of Thy kingdom. O God! Unite us and connect our hearts with Thy indissoluble bond. Verily, Thou art the Giver, Thou art the Kind One and Thou art the Almighty!

'Abdu'l-Bahá

19 *'Alá*   20 *March*

O GOD! O God! From the unseen Kingdom of Thy Oneness behold us assembled in this spiritual meeting, believing in Thee, confident in Thy signs, firm in Thy Covenant and Testament, attracted to Thee, set aglow with the fire of Thy love and sincere in Thy Cause. We are servants in Thy vineyard, spreaders of Thy religion, humble worshippers of Thy countenance, submissive before Thy door and imploring Thee to confirm us in Thy service among Thy chosen ones. Support us with Thine unseen hosts, strengthen our loins in Thy servitude and make us submissive and adoring subjects communing with Thee.

O our Lord! We are weak and Thou art the Mighty, the Powerful! We are mortal and Thou art the great Life-Giving Spirit! We are needy but Thou art the Sustainer and the Powerful!

O our Lord! Turn our faces unto Thy divine face; feed us

from Thy heavenly table with Thine abundant grace; assist us with the hosts of Thy supreme angels, and confirm us through the Holy Ones of the Kingdom of Abhá.

Verily, Thou art the Generous, the Merciful! Thou art the Possessor of great bounty, and verily, Thou art the Clement and the Gracious.

'Abdu'l-Bahá

The Feast of Naw-Rúz and the month of Bahá begin at sunset.

References

Bahá

1. Bahá'u'lláh, *Tablets*, pp. 63–4.
2. ibid. pp. 129–30.
3. Bahá'u'lláh, *Gleanings*, p. 206.
4. ibid. p. 287.
5. ibid. p. 81.
6. Bahá'u'lláh, *Tablets*, p. 125.
7. 'Abdu'l-Bahá, *Promulgation*, pp. 339–40.
8. ibid. p. 364.
9. ibid. p. 365.
10. Bahá'u'lláh, *Gleanings*, pp. 167–8.
11. Bahá'u'lláh, *Tablets*, p. 161.
12. Bahá'u'lláh, *Epistle*, p. 12.
13. Bahá'u'lláh, *Gleanings*, p. 299.
14. 'Abdu'l-Bahá, *Promulgation*, p. 338.
15. ibid. p. 151.
16. Bahá'u'lláh, *Gleanings*, pp. 79–80.
17. 'Abdu'l-Bahá, *Promulgation*, p. 391.
18. 'Abdu'l-Bahá, *Paris Talks*, p. 121.
19. Bahá'u'lláh, *Gleanings*, p. 79.

Jalál

1. The Báb, *Selections*, p. 87.
2. ibid. p. 161.
3. Bahá'u'lláh, *Íqán*, pp. 12–13.
4. The Báb, *Selections*, p. 126.
5. ibid.
6. ibid. pp. 112–13.

231

7. Bahá'u'lláh, *Gleanings*, pp. 74–5.
8. 'Abdu'l-Bahá, *Bahá'í World Faith*, p. 358.
9. The Báb, *Selections*, pp. 105–6.
10. 'Abdu'l-Bahá, *Promulgation*, pp. 126–7.
11. 'Abdu'l-Bahá, *Selections*, p. 207.
12. Bahá'u'lláh, *Íqán*, pp. 106–7.
13. Bahá'u'lláh, *Tablets*, p. 161.
14. Bahá'u'lláh, *Gleanings*, p. 52.
15. 'Abdu'l-Bahá, *Promulgation*, pp. 313–14.
16. ibid. pp. 197–8.
17. ibid. p. 115.
18. ibid. p. 154.
19. The Báb, *Selections*, pp. 110–11.

Jamál

1. The Báb, *Selections*, p. 68.
2. The Báb, *Covenant*, p. 27.
3. The Báb, *Selections*, p. 131.
4. The Báb, *Covenant*, p. 26.
5. ibid. p. 28.
6. ibid. p. 27.
7. The Báb, *Selections*, pp. 156–7.
8. The Báb, *Bahá'í World Faith*, pp. 100–1.
9. The Báb, *Selections*, p. 91.
10. The Báb, *Covenant*, p. 25.
11. The Báb, *Selections*, p. 104.
12. ibid. p. 104.
13. ibid. p. 168.
14. ibid. p. 95.
15. ibid. p. 135.
16. ibid. pp. 167–8.
17. ibid. p. 98.
18. ibid. p. 164.
19. ibid. p. 60.

'Aẓamat

1. Bahá'u'lláh, *Meditations*, p. 306.

2. Bahá'u'lláh, cited in *World Order*, p. 111.
3. Bahá'u'lláh, *Gleanings*, p. 5.
4. Bahá'u'lláh, cited in *World Order*, p. 103.
5. Bahá'u'lláh, *Meditations*. pp. 128–9.
6. The Báb, *Selections*, p. 46.
7. Bahá'u'lláh, *Meditations*, p. 275.
8. Bahá'u'lláh, *Covenant*, pp. 36–7.
9. Bahá'u'lláh, *Gleanings*, pp. 12–13.
10. Bahá'u'lláh, *Tablets*, p. 47.
11. ibid. p. 11.
12. ibid. p. 231.
13. ibid. pp. 114–15.
14. ibid. p. 107.
15. Bahá'u'lláh, *Covenant*, p. 28.
16. Bahá'u'lláh, *Meditations*, pp. 180–1.
17. Bahá'u'lláh, *Epistle*, p. 142.
18. Bahá'u'lláh, *Tablets*, p. 119.
19. 'Abdu'l-Bahá, *Covenant*, p. 63.

Núr

1. Bahá'u'lláh, *Tablets*, p. 3.
2. Bahá'u'lláh, *Gleanings*, p. 28.
3. ibid. p. 197.
4. ibid. pp. 210–11.
5. ibid. p. 39.
6. Bahá'u'lláh, *Tablets*, p. 103.
7. ibid. p. 259.
8. ibid. pp. 258–9.
9. Bahá'u'lláh, *Gleanings*, p. 13.
10. Bahá'u'lláh, cited in *World Order*, p. 167.
11. ibid. p. 107.
12. Bahá'u'lláh, *Tablets*, pp. 107–8.
13. ibid. p. 258.
14. ibid. pp. 78–9.
15. The Báb, *Selections*, p. 161.
16. Bahá'u'lláh, *Gleanings*, pp. 10–11.
17. ibid. p. 163.

18. ibid. p. 245.
19. Bahá'u'lláh, *Meditations*, p. 356.

Raḥmat

1. Bahá'u'lláh, *Gleanings*, p. 194.
2. ibid. pp. 105–6.
3. Bahá'u'lláh, *Tablets*, p. 51.
4. Bahá'u'lláh, *Gleanings*, p. 143.
5. ibid. pp. 106–7.
6. ibid. pp. 86–7.
7. Bahá'u'lláh, *Íqán*, p. 138.
8. Bahá'u'lláh, *Gleanings*, p. 77.
9. Bahá'u'lláh, *Prayers*, p. 4.
10. Bahá'u'lláh, *Gleanings*, p. 293.
11. ibid. p. 261.
12. Bahá'u'lláh, *Persian Hidden Words*, no. 5.
13. Bahá'u'lláh, *Gleanings*, p. 65.
14. ibid. pp. 330–31.
15. ibid. p. 5.
16. Bahá'u'lláh, *Tablets*, p. 268.
17. Bahá'u'lláh, *Gleanings*, p. 289.
18. ibid. p. 332.
19. ibid. p. 333.

Kalimát

1. Bahá'u'lláh, cited in *World Order*, p. 135.
2. Bahá'u'lláh, *Tablets*, pp. 221–2.
3. Bahá'u'lláh, cited in *World Order*, p. 135.
4. ibid.
5. ibid. p. 134
6. Bahá'u'lláh, *Covenant*, p. 62.
7. 'Abdu'l-Bahá, cited in *World Order*, p. 138.
8. 'Abdu'l-Bahá, *Bahá'í World Faith*, pp. 358–9.
9. 'Abdu'l-Bahá, *Promulgation*, pp. 322–3.
10. ibid. p. 323.
11. ibid. p. 382.

12. ibid. p. 386.
13. 'Abdu'l-Bahá, cited in *World Order*, p. 136.
14. 'Abdu'l-Bahá, *Promulgation*, p. 323.
15. ibid. p. 386.
16. 'Abdu'l-Bahá, *The Covenant* (compilation), p. 5.
17. 'Abdu'l-Bahá, *Bahá'í World Faith*, p. 358.
18. ibid.
19. 'Abdu'l-Bahá, *Promulgation*, p. 456.

Kamál

1. 'Abdu'l-Bahá, cited in *World Order*, p. 139.
2. 'Abdu'l-Bahá, *Selections*, p. 295.
3. 'Abdu'l-Bahá, cited in *World Order*, p. 133.
4. ibid. p. 138.
5. Bahá'u'lláh, ibid. pp. 133–6.
6. ibid.
7. ibid.
8. ibid. p. 136.
9. Bahá'u'lláh, *Tablets*, pp. 227–8.
10. Bahá'u'lláh, *Bahá'í World Faith*, p. 437.
11. Bahá'u'lláh, cited in *'Abdu'l-Bahá*, p. 44.
12. ibid. p. 51.
13. 'Abdu'l-Bahá, *Selections*, p. 80.
14. 'Abdu'l-Bahá, *Early Pilgrimage*, pp. 15–16.
15. Bahá'u'lláh, cited in *World Order*, p. 136.
16. Bahá'u'lláh, *Bahá'í World Faith*, p. 436.
17. 'Abdu'l-Bahá, *Will and Testament*.
18. ibid.
19. Bahá'u'lláh, *Bahá'í World Faith*, pp. 436–7.

Asmá'

1. 'Abdu'l-Bahá, *Will and Testament*.
2. 'Abdu'l-Bahá, *Covenant*, p. 99.
3. 'Abdu'l-Bahá, *Will and Testament*.
4. ibid.
5. ibid.

6. 'Abdu'l-Bahá, *Promulgation*, p. 455.
7. 'Abdu'l-Bahá, *Universal House of Justice*, p. 10.
8. Bahá'u'lláh, *Tablets*, p. 93.
9. ibid. p. 128.
10. 'Abdu'l-Bahá, *Will and Testament*.
11. Bahá'u'lláh, *Tablets*, p. 68.
12. 'Abdu'l-Bahá, cited in *Wellspring*, p. 84.
13. Bahá'u'lláh, *Tablets*, p. 129.
14. 'Abdu'l-Bahá, *Universal House of Justice*, p. 11.
15. ibid.
16. 'Abdu'l-Bahá, cited in *Wellspring*, pp. 85–6.
17. Bahá'u'lláh, *Tablets*, p. 125.
18. ibid. pp. 69–70.
19. ibid. p. 89.

'Izzat

1. Bahá'u'lláh, *Covenant*, p. 61.
2. Bahá'u'lláh, cited in *World Order*, p. 132.
3. 'Abdu'l-Bahá, *Selections*, p. 68.
4. ibid. p. 67.
5. 'Abdu'l-Bahá, cited in *World Order*, p. 167.
6. 'Abdu'l-Bahá, *Selections*, p. 67.
7. 'Abdu'l-Bahá, *Universal House of Justice*, p. 10.
8. ibid. p. 12.
9. 'Abdu'l-Bahá, *Selections*, p. 67.
10. 'Abdu'l-Bahá, cited in *World Order*, p. 111.
11. Bahá'u'lláh, ibid. p. 116.
12. ibid. p. 117.
13. ibid.
14. ibid. p. 116.
15. Bahá'u'lláh, *Gleanings*, pp. 268–70.
16. The Báb, *Selections*, p. 144.
17. Bahá'u'lláh, *Gleanings*, pp. 73–4.
18. ibid. pp. 68–9.
19. Bahá'u'lláh, cited in *World Order*, p. 116.

Mashíyyat

1. Bahá'u'lláh, *Gleanings*, pp. 336–7.
2. ibid. p. 174.
3. ibid. p. 175.
4. ibid. p. 66.
5. Bahá'u'lláh, *Covenant*, p. 51.
6. 'Abdu'l-Bahá, *Paris Talks*, p. 32.
7. ibid. p. 57.
8. ibid. p. 18.
9. 'Abdu'l-Bahá, *Power of the Covenant*, part 2, p. 9.
10. The Báb, *Selections*, p. 65.
11. 'Abdu'l-Bahá, *Bahá'í World Faith*, p. 429.
12. 'Abdu'l-Bahá, cited in *God Passes By*, p. 238.
13. Bahá'u'lláh, ibid.
14. ibid.
15. 'Abdu'l-Bahá, *The Covenant, Its Meaning*, p. 76.
16. 'Abdu'l-Bahá, *Selections*, p. 223.
17. 'Abdu'l-Bahá, cited in *Light of 'Akká*, p. 48.
18. 'Abdu'l-Bahá, *Selections*, p. 216.
19. 'Abdu'l-Bahá, *Power of the Covenant*, p. 58.

'Ilm

1. Bahá'u'lláh, *Gleanings*, p. 286.
2. ibid. p. 97.
3. Bahá'u'lláh, cited in *World Order*, p. 25.
4. Bahá'u'lláh, *Gleanings*, p. 286.
5. ibid. p. 243.
6. Bahá'u'lláh, *Tablets*, p. 162.
7. 'Abdu'l-Bahá, *Bahá'í World Faith*, p. 402.
8. 'Abdu'l-Bahá, *Paris Talks*, p. 130.
9. 'Abdu'l-Bahá, *Selections*, p. 209.
10. 'Abdu'l-Bahá, *Promulgation*, pp. 455–6.
11. ibid. p. 456.
12. ibid. p. 317.
13. ibid. p. 386.
14. ibid.

15. 'Abdu'l-Bahá, *Divine Plan*, p. 49.
16. 'Abdu'l-Bahá, *Selections*, p. 19.
17. 'Abdu'l-Bahá, *Divine Plan*, p. 49.
18. 'Abdu'l-Bahá, *Selections*, p. 215.
19. Bahá'u'lláh, *Covenant*, p. 59.

Qudrat

1. 'Abdu'l-Bahá, *Will and Testament*.
2. 'Abdu'l-Bahá, *Covenant*, p. 70.
3. 'Abdu'l-Bahá, cited in *God Passes By*, p. 238.
4. 'Abdu'l-Bahá, *Divine Plan*, p. 49.
5. 'Abdu'l-Bahá, cited in *God Passes By*, p. 239.
6. 'Abdu'l-Bahá, *Selections*, pp. 102–3.
7. ibid. pp. 208–9.
8. ibid. p. 223.
9. ibid. p. 228.
10. 'Abdu'l-Bahá, *Divine Plan*, p. 49.
11. Bahá'u'lláh, *Tablets*, p. 221.
12. 'Abdu'l-Bahá, *Bahá'í World Faith*, pp. 357–8.
13. 'Abdu'l-Bahá, *Covenant*, p. 71.
14. 'Abdu'l-Bahá, *Power of the Covenant*, part 2, p. 47.
15. 'Abdu'l-Bahá, *The Covenant* (compilation), p. 17.
16. 'Abdu'l-Bahá, cited in *World Order*, p. 17.
17. 'Abdu'l-Bahá, *Selections*, pp. 210–11.
18. Bahá'u'lláh, cited in *Advent*, p. 69.
19. 'Abdu'l-Bahá, *Bahá'í World Faith*, p. 363.

Qawl

1. Bahá'u'lláh, *Gleanings*, p. 290.
2. ibid.
3. Bahá'u'lláh, *Women*, p. 23.
4. 'Abdu'l-Bahá, *Bahá'í World Faith*, p. 359.
5. 'Abdu'l-Bahá, *Selections*, pp. 25–6.
6. 'Abdu'l-Bahá, *Early Pilgrimage*, pp. 12–13.
7. 'Abdu'l-Bahá, *Divine Plan*, p. 49.

8. 'Abdu'l-Bahá, *Bahá'í World Faith*, p. 363.
9. 'Abdu'l-Bahá, *Promulgation*, p. 381.
10. Bahá'u'lláh, *Tablets*, pp. 181–2.
11. 'Abdu'l-Bahá, *Power of the Covenant*, part 2, p. 48.
12. ibid. p. 33.
13. Bahá'u'lláh, *Gleanings*, p. 328.
14. Bahá'u'lláh, *Epistle*, pp. 146–7.
15. 'Abdu'l-Bahá, *Bahá'í World Faith*, p. 434.
16. 'Abdu'l-Bahá, *Selections*, p. 211.
17. ibid. p. 210.
18. ibid. p. 250.
19. ibid. p. 26.

Masá'il

1. Bahá'u'lláh, *Tablets*, p. 17.
2. Bahá'u'lláh, *Gleanings*, p. 9.
3. Bahá'u'lláh, *Covenant*, p. 140.
4. 'Abdu'l-Bahá, *Selections*, p. 85.
5. Bahá'u'lláh, *Tablets*, p. 120.
6. The Báb, *Selections*, p. 52.
7. Bahá'u'lláh, *Tablets*, p. 220.
8. Bahá'u'lláh, *Gleanings*, pp. 245–6.
9. Bahá'u'lláh, *Tablets*, pp. 58–9.
10. ibid. p. 220.
11. Bahá'u'lláh, *Covenant*, p. 140.
12. Bahá'u'lláh, *Gleanings*, p. 330.
13. 'Abdu'l-Bahá, *Selections*, p. 212.
14. ibid. p. 209.
15. Bahá'u'lláh, *Tablets*, p. 90.
16. 'Abdu'l-Bahá, *Selections*, pp. 85–6.
17. ibid. p. 89.
18. ibid. p. 23.
19. ibid. p. 309.

Sharaf

1. Bahá'u'lláh, *Gleanings*, p. 337.

2. Bahá'u'lláh, *Deepening*, p. 3.
3. ibid. p. 1.
4. Bahá'u'lláh, *Gleanings*, p. 7.
5. Bahá'u'lláh, *Persian Hidden Words*, no. 64.
6. 'Abdu'l-Bahá, *Selections*, p. 71.
7. ibid. p. 203.
8. 'Abdu'l-Bahá, *Excellence in All Things*, pp. 6–7.
9. ibid. p. 7.
10. ibid. pp. 7–8.
11. Bahá'u'lláh, *Bahá'í Education*, p. 8.
12. 'Abdu'l-Bahá, cited in *Bahá'í Administration*, p. 36.
13. 'Abdu'l-Bahá, *Bahá'í World Faith*, p. 437.
14. Bahá'u'lláh, *Divorce*, p. 5.
15. 'Abdu'l-Bahá, *Paris Talks*, pp. 148–9.
16. Bahá'u'lláh, *Gleanings*, p. 331.
17. 'Abdu'l-Bahá, *Promulgation*, pp. 323–4.
18. 'Abdu'l-Bahá, *Selections*, pp. 243–6.
19. 'Abdu'l-Bahá, cited in *'Abdu'l-Bahá*, pp. 405–6.

Sulṭán

1. Bahá'u'lláh, *Meditations*, p. 284.
2. Bahá'u'lláh, *Tablets*, pp. 102–3.
3. 'Abdu'l-Bahá, cited in *New Era*, p. 130.
4. Bahá'u'lláh, *Covenant*, p. 140.
5. 'Abdu'l-Bahá, ibid. p. 110.
6. Bahá'u'lláh, *Arabic Hidden Words*, no. 71.
7. Bahá'u'lláh, *Covenant*, p. 141.
8. ibid. p. 140.
9. 'Abdu'l-Bahá, *Selections*, p. 214.
10. 'Abdu'l-Bahá, *Covenant*, p. 132.
11. 'Abdu'l-Bahá, *Promulgation*, p. 382.
12. 'Abdu'l-Bahá, *Selections*, pp. 213, 214.
13. 'Abdu'l-Bahá, *Power of the Covenant*, part 2, p. 34.
14. 'Abdu'l-Bahá, *Covenant*, p. 134.
15. ibid. p. 111.
16. Bahá'u'lláh, *Power of the Covenant*, part 2, p. 10.
17. 'Abdu'l-Bahá, ibid. part 2, p. 10.

18. Bahá'u'lláh, *Covenant*, p. 141.
19. 'Abdu'l-Bahá, *Seeking the Light*, p. 26.

Mulk

1. Bahá'u'lláh, *Íqán*, p. 6.
2. The Báb, cited in *World Order*, p. 101.
3. Bahá'u'lláh, *Gleanings*, p. 329.
4. Bahá'u'lláh, cited in *World Order*, p. 109.
5. Bahá'u'lláh, cited in *Advent*, p. 69.
6. 'Abdu'l-Bahá, *Crisis and Victory*, p. 25.
7. 'Abdu'l-Bahá, cited in *World Order*, p. 17.
8. 'Abdu'l-Bahá, *Power of the Covenant*, part 2, p. 58.
9. 'Abdu'l-Bahá, *Promulgation*, pp. 428–30.
10. 'Abdu'l-Bahá, *Onward March*, p. 7.
11. ibid.
12. 'Abdu'l-Bahá, *Selections*, p. 74.
13. ibid. pp. 9–10.
14. Bahá'u'lláh, *Crisis and Victory*, p. 42.
15. Bahá'u'lláh, *Epistle*, p. 147.
16. 'Abdu'l-Bahá, *Selections*, p. 227.
17. ibid. p. 233.
18. Bahá'u'lláh, *Gleanings*, p. 319.
19. 'Abdu'l-Bahá, *Will and Testament*.

Ayyám-i-Há

1. Bahá'u'lláh, *Women*, pp. 1–2.
2. 'Abdu'l-Bahá, *Selections*, p. 208.
3. ibid. p. 255.
4. 'Abdu'l-Bahá, *Bahá'í World Faith*, pp. 362–3.
5. 'Abdu'l-Bahá, cited in *Wellspring*, p. 127.

'Alá

1. Bahá'u'lláh, *Meditations*, p. 106.
2. The Báb, *Selections*, p. 315.
3. Bahá'u'lláh, *Bahá'í Prayers* (UK), pp. 48–9.

4. 'Abdu'l-Bahá, *Prayers*, pp. 71–2.
5. Bahá'u'lláh, *Bahá'í Prayers* (UK), p. 18.
6. 'Abdu'l-Bahá, *Selections*, p. 259.
7. Bahá'u'lláh, *Prayers*, pp. 69–70.
8. 'Abdu'l-Bahá, ibid. pp. 70–1.
9. Bahá'u'lláh, ibid. pp. 68–9.
10. 'Abdu'l-Bahá, *Will and Testament*.
11. Bahá'u'lláh, *Bahá'í Prayers* (UK), p. 17.
12. 'Abdu'l-Bahá, *Covenant*, p. 83.
13. Bahá'u'lláh, *Bahá'í Prayers* (UK), p. 60.
14. 'Abdu'l-Bahá, ibid. pp. 96–7.
15. Bahá'u'lláh, ibid. pp. 59–60.
16. 'Abdu'l-Bahá, ibid. pp. 79–80.
17. Bahá'u'lláh, *Meditations*, p. 174.
18. 'Abdu'l-Bahá, *Bahá'í Prayers* (UK), p. 90.
19. ibid. p. 98.

Bibliography

'Abdu'l-Bahá. *Paris Talks*. Oakham: Bahá'í Publishing Trust, 1972.

—— *The Promulgation of Universal Peace*. Wilmette, Illinois: Bahá'í Publishing Trust, 1982.

—— *Tablets of the Divine Plan*. Wilmette, Illinois: Bahá'í Publishing Trust, 1977.

—— *Will and Testament of 'Abdu'l-Bahá*. Wilmette, Illinois: Bahá'í Publishing Trust, 1944.

Báb, The. *Selections from the Writings of the Báb*. Compiled by the Research Department of the Universal House of Justice and translated by Habib Taherzadeh with the assistance of a Committee at the Bahá'í World Centre. Haifa: Bahá'í World Centre, 1976.

Bahá'í Education. Compilation issued by the Universal House of Justice. Oakham: Bahá'í Publishing Trust, 1976.

Bahá'í Prayers. Oakham: Bahá'í Publishing Trust, 1967.

Bahá'í Prayers. Wilmette, Illinois: Bahá'í Publishing Trust, 1982.

Bahá'í World Faith. Wilmette, Illinois: Bahá'í Publishing Trust, rev. ed., 1976.

Bahá'u'lláh. *Epistle to the Son of the Wolf*. Wilmette, Illinois: Bahá'í Publishing Trust, 1962.

—— *Gleanings from the Writings of Bahá'u'lláh*. Translated by Shoghi Effendi. Wilmette, Illinois: Bahá'í Publishing Trust, 1963.

—— *The Hidden Words of Bahá'u'lláh*. Wilmette, Illinois: Bahá'í Publishing Trust, 1954.

243

—— *Kitáb-i-Íqán: The Book of Certitude*. Wilmette, Illinois: Bahá'í Publishing Trust, 1960.

—— *Prayers and Meditations*. Wilmette, Illinois: Bahá'í Publishing Trust, 1969.

—— *Tablets of Bahá'u'lláh revealed after the Kitáb-i-Aqdas*. Compiled by the Research Department of the Universal House of Justice and translated by Habib Taherzadeh with the assistance of a Committee at the Bahá'í World Centre. Haifa: Bahá'í World Centre, 1978.

Balyuzi, H. M. *'Abdu'l-Bahá*. Oxford, George Ronald, 1971.

Covenant, The. Compilation issued by the Universal House of Justice. Oakham: Bahá'í Publishing Trust, 1988.

Covenant, The: Its Meaning and Origin and Our Attitude Toward It. Wilmette, Illinois: National Teaching Committee of the National Spiritual Assembly of the Bahá'ís of the United States, 1988.

Covenant of Bahá'u'lláh, The. London: Bahá'í Publishing Trust, 1963.

Crisis and Victory. Compilation issued by the Universal House of Justice. Oakham: Bahá'í Publishing Trust, 1988.

Deepening. Compilation issued by the Universal House of Justice. Oakham: Bahá'í Publishing Trust, 1983.

Divorce. Compilation issued by the Universal House of Justice. Oakham: Bahá'í Publishing Trust, 1986.

Esslemont, J. E. *Bahá'u'llah and the New Era*. Wilmette, Illinois: Bahá'í Publishing Trust, 4th rev. ed. 1976.

Excellence in All Things. Compilation issued by the Universal House of Justice. Oakham: Bahá'í Publishing Trust, 1981.

Grundy, Julia M. *Ten Days in the Light of 'Akká*. Wilmette, Illinois: Bahá'í Publishing Trust, 1979.

Maxwell, May. *An Early Pilgrimage*. Oxford: George Ronald, 1969.

Onward March of the Faith, The. Compilation issued by the Universal House of Justice. Oakham: Bahá'í Publishing Trust, 1975.

Power of the Covenant, The. National Spiritual Assembly of the Bahá'ís of Canada. September 1977.

Seeking the Light of the Kingdom. Compilation issued by the

Universal House of Justice. Oakham: Bahá'í Publishing Trust, 1977.

Shoghi Effendi. *The Advent of Divine Justice*. Wilmette, Illinois: Bahá'í Publishing Trust, 1963.

—— *Bahá'í Administration: Selected Messages 1922–1932*. Wilmette, Illinois: Bahá'í Publishing Trust, 1974.

—— *God Passes By*. Wilmette, Illinois: Bahá'í Publishing Trust, 1944.

—— *The World Order of Bahá'u'lláh*. Wilmette, Illinois: Bahá'í Publishing Trust, 1955.

Universal House of Justice. *Wellspring of Guidance*. Wilmette, Illinois: Bahá'í Publishing Trust, 1969.

Universal House of Justice, The. Compilation issued by the Universal House of Justice. Oakham: Bahá'í Publishing Trust, 1987.

Women. Compilation issued by the Universal House of Justice. Oakham: Bahá'í Publishing Trust, 1986.